| OX | 05/19 | | | | | |

C000182199

To renew this book, phone 0845 1202811 or visit
our website at www.libcat.oxfordshire.gov.uk
You will need your library PIN number
(available from your library)

OXFORDSHIRE
COUNTY COUNCIL
SOCIAL & COMMUNITY SERVICES
www.oxfordshire.gov.uk

3303482379

By the same author:

SOLDIER OF THE RAJ

ADMIRAL OF THE BLUE

BLOODLINE

LIFELINE

THE NIGHT HUNTER'S PREY

Novels:

EASTER AT THE VILLA VICTORIA

IRENE

IAIN GORDON is a retired publisher and writer
whose work on military history is read throughout
the English-speaking world.

IAIN GORDON

Rebel with a Cause

The Life and Times of
Sarah Benett (1850-1924)
Social Reformer and Suffragette

PEN & SWORD
HISTORY

AN IMPRINT OF PEN & SWORD BOOKS LTD.
YORKSHIRE – PHILADELPHIA

First published in Great Britain in 2018 by
Pen & Sword History
An imprint of
Pen & Sword Books Ltd
Yorkshire – Philadelphia

Copyright © Iain Gordon, 2018

HB ISBN 978 1 52674 170 7
PB ISBN 978 1 52675 150 8

The right of Iain Gordon to be identified as Author of this work has been asserted
by him in accordance with the Copyright, Designs and Patents Act 1988.

A CIP catalogue record for this book is
available from the British Library.

Printed and bound in England by TJ International Ltd, Padstow, Cornwall.

Pen & Sword Books Limited incorporates the imprints of Atlas, Archaeology,
Aviation, Discovery, Family History, Fiction, History, Maritime, Military,
Military Classics, Politics, Select, Transport, True Crime, Air World, Frontline
Publishing, Leo Cooper, Remember When, Seaforth Publishing, The Praetorian
Press, Wharncliffe Local History, Wharncliffe Transport, Wharncliffe True
Crime and White Owl.

For ... ntact

47 Chu... ... England

E. ... ...m

Contents

List of Illustrations

Illustrations

Preface

This book has no pretensions to scholarship; it is a simple tale, simply told, of a brave and determined woman, the times in which she lived and the people with whom she worked. I have not, therefore, laboured the text with references and have kept footnotes to a minimum. I have been fortunate in having been given access to Sarah Benett's prison memoirs and private papers but, apart from these, there is nothing in this book which has not been previously published – much of it many, many times. There can surely be few civil events in history which have received such attention as the suffragettes and their fight for women's rights. Hundreds of books have been written covering every aspect of the subject; every prominent protagonist, every phase of the battle and every individual incident has been exhaustively studied by experts, analysed and recorded; many suffragists have left unpublished memoirs of their activities; published biographies and autobiographies abound.

So, for anyone who seeks a scholarly study of the fight for women's suffrage, or of any specific aspect of it, with learned analysis of every campaigner's achievements and the source of every fact and reference recorded, there is no shortage of works and I have included a short index of a few of the most important at the back of this book. This book, I hope, will appeal to general readers unfamiliar with the subject who merely want a superficial overview of the period with a personal insight into the aspirations and activities of one of the lesser-known fighters for women's rights.

It is almost inconceivable today that, a mere 100 years ago, the opinion of a woman with a university degree should have been regarded as being of less value than that of an illiterate manual worker; that women should be excluded from some political meetings; excluded from standing for Parliament; excluded from any activity which might dare to suggest that they were on a level with men in terms of intelligence and ability. Something had to be done and in 1817 the battle began to redress one of the greatest social injustices of modern times. Little was achieved for the first 80 years until the suffragettes, with their aggressive campaigning and militant tactics, brought the issue to the attention of a public, the larger part of which had never paused to consider the gross oppression of one half of the population of Britain which the system perpetuated.

They came from stately homes and from miners' cottages; from Scotland, England, Wales and Ireland; their ages ranged from 18 to 80; some had never known hunger others had never known a full stomach. A more diverse conglomerate would be difficult to find yet the cause for which they fought was so noble that it formed them readily into an unwavering sisterhood.

At the time, the suffragettes probably made as many enemies as friends and the women had to suffer ridicule, abuse and physical hardship in their struggle for recognition. Many never lived to see the complete fulfilment of their aspirations with the introduction of universal suffrage. But, even in the first decade of the twentieth century, activists were able to see cracks appearing in the bedrock of prejudice and those with faith must have known that one day the battle would be won, even if they were not around to enjoy the equality that victory would achieve.

There were, of course, families, like the Pankhursts, where every member rallied to the cause, but in the great majority of respectable households, at every level of the social scale, for a female member to leave home and join up with a band of boisterous, law-breaking revolutionaries, as they were generally perceived, brought deep shame upon the family and often resulted in a rift which might never heal. So as well as possessing the courage to face injury, imprisonment and public contempt, the suffragette had to be prepared for the loneliness and isolation which might result from her excommunication by family and friends. It would be some years before families would start to be proud of, instead of embarrassed by, their capricious suffragette members.

Opinions were strongly held and differed widely. Several attempts were made to construct a single, unified body which would speak with one voice but this was never achieved. Splinter groups formed their own organisations and members were wont to move from one group to another, and often back again, as the policies of the group developed and their own convictions matured. The most elemental difference of opinion was between those who believed that their actions should always be within the law and those who believed that the end would justify the means. As it appeared to the latter that lawful agitation had achieved nothing, they believed that the only way to get results was by unlawful behaviour to which they consequently applied themselves.

There were men, too, who shared the passionate commitment of the women though not all of the groups would admit men and there were Members of Parliament who were not unsympathetic to the cause though their active support was often constricted by other political considerations. Men and women who advocated extension of the suffrage to women were known as suffragists; the term 'suffragettes', first used in the *'Daily Mail'* and then universally adopted as a flippant and patronising form of address, was seized upon with delight by the women themselves and has thus passed into the English language. The 'Women's Social and Political Union' (WSPU) even called their newspaper *'The Suffragette'* in which they included their own explanation of the difference between the two words: " . . . *[the] Suffragist just wants the vote, while the Suffragette means to get it."* Today, with the constraint upon gender specific suffixes such as -ette and -ess, the word 'Suffragette' proudly withstands demands for an impoverished, politically correct, alternative.

Sarah Benett was unequivocally a 'Suffragette' despite a brief flirtation with the more placid 'Women's Freedom League' of which she was Treasurer for a time. She was an educated woman with strong convictions, which she was not afraid to air, which tended to brand her as 'difficult' and may have prejudiced her chances of gaining high office in the movement. Nevertheless, she played her full part in all its activities as a dedicated foot soldier – demonstrating, breaking windows, serving time in prison and, at the age of 62, being one of only six women who completed a gruelling 400 mile march from Edinburgh to London to show the flag and spread the word. She was the perfect affirmation of the WSPU motto *"Actions not Words"* and there can be little doubt that, like so many other suffragettes, her spirited lifestyle had a detrimental effect upon her health.

This year, 2018, is a particularly appropriate year in which to examine the work and achievements of the women who fought for the right to vote; it is the centenary of the *Representation of the People Act 1918* which extended the franchise to women over 30 years of age. The electorate was tripled and women comprised 42% of it. It would be another 10 years before true universal suffrage was achieved but this was the first major battle which the women had won. They had a voice at last.

It is also the centenary of the *Parliament (Qualification of Women) Act 1918* which gave women over 21 the right to stand for election to Parliament and, the following year, Nancy Astor became the first woman to sit at Westminster. There could be no turning back now.

Mrs. Emmeline Pankhurst had earlier written:

> *"The militancy of men, through all the centuries, has drenched the world with blood, and for these deeds of horror and destruction men have been rewarded with monuments, with great songs and epics. The militancy of women has harmed no human life save the lives of those who fought the battle of righteousness. Time alone will reveal what reward will be allotted to women."*

Time has indeed revealed the rewards for the actions of the suffragettes the most readily identifiable of which must surely be the preeminent positions of power that women occupy today in the hierarchy of the western world and at the apex of every field and profession. Yet there are those who consider that this is not enough and that women are still unjustly oppressed. They believe that the structure of the social order should be contrived and that the selection of the best people for any specific role, regardless of sex, should be overruled by enforced gender quotients. They do not always get their own way so they believe that *"the fight must go on"*.

I rather feel that Sarah Benett might have agreed with them.

Iain Gordon
Barnstaple, Devon
September 2018

Abbreviations

AFL	Actresses Franchise League
aka	Also known as (pseudonym)
BMA	British Medical Association
CLAW	Control of Lead at Work (Regulations)
CND	Campaign for Nuclear Disarmament
ELFS	East London Federation of Suffragettes
HMS	His/Her Majesty's Ship
ICWPP	International Committee of Women for Permanent Peace
IFFF	*Internationale Frau Enlisa fur Frieden und Freihest* (International Women's League for Peace and Liberty)
ILP	Independent Labour Party
KC	King's Counsel (senior barrister)
MP	Member of Parliament
NSS	National Secular Society
NLOWS	National League for Opposing Woman Suffrage
NSWS	National Society for Women's Suffrage
NUWSS	National Union of Women's Suffrage Societies
NHS	National Health Service
PM	Prime Minister
RN	Royal Navy
SPCA	Society for the Prevention of Cruelty to Animals
SS	Steam Ship
VAD	Voluntary Aid Detachment (temporary nurses)
WCG	Women's Cooperative Guild
WFL	Women's Freedom League
	Women's Franchise League
WILFF	Women's International League for Peace and Freedom
WNASL	Women's National Anti-Suffrage League
WSPU	Women's Social and Political Union
WTRL	Women's Tax Resistance League
WVS	Women's Voluntary Service

BUILDING NEWS 12 DECEMBER 1879

Anderton's Hotel after its 1879/80 rebuild.

1. Breakfast Meeting

Anderton's Hotel, 162-165 Fleet Street, London.
January 1907

Anderton's Hotel could lay claim to being the oldest tavern in Fleet Street, quite possibly in the whole of London. It had been established in 1385 as 'The Horn in the Hoop' later changed to 'The Horn Tavern' and on the death of its goldsmith proprietor, Thomas Atte Hay, in 1405, it had passed, by his bequest, into the ownership of The Goldsmiths' Company *"for the better support and sustenation of the infirm members of the Company."* Five hundred years later, in 1905, it was still in the same ownership.

Opposite: **Sarah Benett**
PURVIS FAMILY PAPERS

In 1879/80 the tavern had been completely rebuilt and renamed 'Anderton's Hotel' (though the identity of Mr. Anderton was not recorded). It was described in 1891 as: *"a lofty Queen Anne building of red brick, stone and granite, one of the showiest edifices in Fleet Street."* [1]

In its new and grand form, the hotel began to attract groups and associations as a venue for their meetings, including such august bodies as the 'National Association of Probation Officers', and in 1906, to cater for this growing demand, the management had undertaken major alterations on the ground floor – the chief of which was to convert the billiard room to a dining room so the old dining room could be fitted out as a spacious and impressive meeting room.

Among the groups which were attracted to Anderton's was the 'Women's Social and Political Union' (WSPU) which had been formed in Manchester in 1903 by Mrs. Emmeline Pankhurst and her daughters Christabel and Sylvia. This organisation was dedicated to the cause of suffrage for women and followed a succession of previous groups all of which had sought change by non-militant and legal campaigning; they had achieved nothing. Mrs. Pankhurst believed that the only way to advance the cause was with high-profile, militant action and in the previous year the first such action, resulting in the arrest and imprisonment of two of the Union's members, had set the mark for the succession of violent acts and demonstrations which were to follow.

The first WSPU prisoners to be released from jail in January 1907 were fêted with a lavish Christmas dinner at the Holborn Restaurant provided by Mr. and Mrs. Pethick-Lawrence, notable supporters of the cause. Later batches of released prisoners were honoured with a more modest breakfast meeting, many being held at Anderton's Hotel.

It was at one such meeting, in January 1907, that Sarah Benett, a 57 year-old woman, recently arrived in London from her home in the Midlands, sat quietly in a row near the back of the hall listening intently to the speaker whose words were to change the course of her life.

The speaker was Flora McKinnon Drummond, known within the Movement as 'The General' due to her propensity for wearing a military

Above: **Sir Henry Campbell-Bannerman 1836-1908**

Left: **Flora Mckinnon Drummond – 'The General' 1878-1949.**

style peaked cap and gold epaulettes. She would take part in demonstrations mounted on a large black horse.

Born in Manchester in 1878, the daughter of a tailor, Flora had felt deeply about the inequalities in society from an early age and, with her upholsterer husband, Joseph, had been an active member of the 'Fabian Society' and the 'Independent Labour Party' (ILP) before joining the WSPU in 1906. She was noted for her ingenuity and daring and told her enthralled audience at Anderton's of how, in March 1906, she had managed to force her way into No. 10 Downing Street while her fellow-protester was being subdued by police on the doorstep. Both of the women had been arrested but had avoided imprisonment as the Prime Minister, Sir Henry Campbell-Bannerman, had refused to press charges. Later in the year she had been imprisoned following a disturbance outside the House of Commons and she served her first of several sentences in Holloway Prison, her release from which was the subject of this particular breakfast meeting.

Sarah Benett had clearly been impressed by Mrs. Drummond's presentation and later wrote:

> *"I forget who was in the Chair, but the chief speaker was Mrs. Drummond who had just been released and whose speech was amusing and inspiring. I felt that her pluck and insolence were quite the right thing; it was one way of breaking down the traditional tone of thought about women and showing the world that it was not of primary importance that women should be pretty or pleasing to men; that was only one phase of life. The important thing was that they should be effective individuals."* [2]

Sarah had for long been toying with the idea of joining an active branch of the suffrage movement. For the past twelve years living, by choice, in the Staffordshire Potteries – one of the unhealthiest and most socially deprived industrial areas in Britain – she had struggled to gain a position where she might have the influence to inaugurate changes in health, education and living standards. Despite the fact that she was an intelligent and well educated person, her ambitions were constantly thwarted, often by those whom she sought to help, simply because she was a woman. Her thoughts were therefore becoming increasingly set upon the fundamental need to redress the injustice of women's place in society before progress could be made in other needful areas.

During 1905 she had worked hard, and with considerable success, to secure signatures on a suffrage petition which had subsequently been ignored by the authorities. With this, and her failure to make any real progress during her twelve years in the Potteries, she started to believe that all forms of peaceful representation were futile and that militant action was the only effective path towards change.

> *"There are three parties in every industrial district, the Church (or conservatives) the Nonconformists (or liberals) and what is picturesquely known as 'Labour'; I will not enlarge upon*

the inappropriateness of the title. Since then labour has taken up the task of fighting its so-called leaders who stand revealed (broadly speaking) as a motley crew of self-seekers drawn from every class and representing themselves primarily.

"I had begun by thinking if I worked hard with trade unionists and cooperators, I should be serving the poor and suffering masses – but those dreams had long been shattered and it had become clear to me that something barred the way to my working hard at anything, and that that something was my sex.

"Those who ran the three parties (shall I say the caucus of each) had had to move with the times; women taking university degrees and entering the professions could no longer be excluded from local governing bodies when the roughest, commonest, self-made men predominated on such bodies. But woe to the woman who would not tolerate wrong doing if she had not others like herself to work with, or a strong social backing. She was mercilessly tricked or persecuted and her position made unbearable. Such was my experience as the 'Labour' member of Burslem School Board and, in 1902, the 'School Act' took from women the right of election. After that they could only be coopted and I was not coopted. I stood for the Town Council in October 1907 but the trades unionists did not care for me to win and, of course, I did not. I had gained the affections of the people, my name was a household word from end to end of the Potteries and I knew that I could have done work which no one else could. Do you wonder that I came to the conclusion that the most pressing question of the day was the position of women; that the sex barrier must be broken down and that this would never be done by talking or petitioning." (2)

The birth of the WSPU had been painful and protracted. Throughout the 19th century, groups and associations had been forming in many parts of the country, all with the objective of pressing for parliamentary reform of women's rights.

Prior to 1832, the right to vote in parliamentary elections was restricted to men of means who were substantial owners of land or property. The *First Reform Act* of 1832 extended the right to men who paid rates on property of a certain value which they rented in rural constituency boroughs; The *Second Reform Act* of 1867 included men in urban areas who met the same property qualifications but women, as had always been the case, were specifically excluded.

Before the 1867 *Reform Act*, two of the leading women's groups, the 'Kensington Society' and the 'Manchester Committee for the Enfranchisement of Women', presented a petition to John Stuart Mill and Henry Fawcett, two radical Members of Parliament who were known to be sympathetic to women's rights. The petition asking for women to be given the vote bore the signatures of nearly 1,500 women. An amendment was consequently added to the Act by Mill to give women the same voting rights as men.

During the ensuing debate, Edward Karslake, a barrister by profession, who was Conservative MP for Colchester, voiced the hackneyed opinion,

Henry Fawcett *(left)* **and John Stuart Mill who were sympathetic to women's rights and presented the amendment to the 1867 Reform Act.**

which was held by a great many men at the time, that women had no interest in political matters and really did not want the vote. He told the House that he had not found a single woman in his constituency who was in favour of votes for women. Though this was swiftly rebutted by the suffragists, who presented a petition signed by 129 women in Karslake's Colchester constituency who supported Mill's amendment, it was nevertheless defeated by 196 votes to 73.

The 1884 *Representation of the People Act* extended to men in rural areas the same rights which the 1837 Act had given their urban counterparts. At this point some 60% of all men could vote in elections.

As far as women were concerned, the *Municipal Franchise Act* of 1869 had given the right to vote, in local elections only, to single women who were ratepayers, and certain married women obtained the same in the 1894 *Local Government Act*. However, the great majority of British women were still denied the basic rights now enjoyed by the majority of men.

The disappointing rejection of Mill's amendment in 1867 had hardened attitudes among suffragists and had resulted in several of the best established women's suffrage groups, mainly from the industrial centres, amalgamating in November 1867 to form the 'National Society for Women's Suffrage' (NSWS). This was the first national organisation to campaign for women's enfranchisement which, it was hoped, would present a far stronger representation of the Movement.

However, internal bickering over differences of opinion in policy, notably whether men should be admitted as members, was to blight the new association from the start; its purpose was weakened and disillusioned members began to fall away and form their own groups. After twenty-one stormy and largely unproductive years the NSWS fractured under the strain and split into two, easily confused, parts – 'The National Central Society for Women's Suffrage' and the remnants of the original body now called the 'Central Committee of the National Society for Women's Suffrage'.

The bickering in the NSWS continued and the following year, in 1889, barrister Richard Pankhurst and his wife Emmeline split off and formed the radical 'Women's Franchise League' which intended to press for an inclusive package of women's rights, including inheritance and divorce, in addition to its central demand for the right to vote. The WFL sought

Mrs. Emmeline Pankhurst who, together with her husband Richard, formed the Women's Franchise League in 1889.

alliances with the Trades Unions and several socialist groups and was consequently considered to be too left-wing by many of the Movement's supporters. A bitter antagonism grew up between the two factions with each publicly insulting the other which did nothing for their cause and provided great amusement to the anti-women's suffrage lobby whose contention that women could never work together in harmony was seen to be not without

Mrs. Millicent Garrett Fawcett, first President of the National Union of Women's Suffrage Societies.

substance. Following an undignified slanging match at an NSWS meeting in St. James's Hall, several important members of the WFL resigned and the group dissolved soon after, about a year after its inception. This was the end of Mrs. Pankhurst's first attempt to launch an effective group to fight for women's suffrage and it was to be another thirteen years before she was able to raise another.

The final attempt in the 19th century to create a unified voice for women's suffrage had been in 1897 with the amalgamation of 'The National Central Society for Women's Suffrage' and 'The Central Committee of the National Society for Women's Suffrage' to form the 'National Union of Women's Suffrage Societies' (NUWSS). Its first President was Millicent Garrett Fawcett, wife of Henry Fawcett MP, and the aim of the Union was to advance the cause by peaceful and legal means.

Membership of the NUWSS was open to men as well as women, its structure was democratic and it had no alliance with any political party. In elections, the Union was pledged to support whichever candidate was supportive of women's suffrage.

Though membership of the NUWSS grew steadily over the next few years, it had achieved little in its mission to convert politicians to its cause by oratory and other peaceful means. Some of the more active members became frustrated with the lack of progress and so it was that, in 1903, Mrs. Pankhurst had re-entered the arena and, together with her daughters, had founded the 'Women's Social and Political Union' WSPU with the object of pursuing the cause by more active means.

The original intention was that the WSPU would work in association with the Independent Labour Party, but

Annie Kenney, a former mill girl who became one of the WSPU's most prominent members.

WIKIPEDIA – AUTHOR UNKNOWN

Sir John Bamford Slack MP

a fundamental difference in the aims of the two organisations, with respect to women's suffrage, soon became apparent: Mrs. Pankhurst's stated aim was to obtain for women the same rights as men enjoyed which, at that time, was restricted to about one-third of the male population and was dependent upon property qualifications. The policy of the ILP, on the other hand, called for universal suffrage for all – both men and women.

This led to a growing perception of the WSPU as an elitist organisation, comprised of upper- and middle-class women who were only concerned with the advancement of their own social group. However, in 1905 the movement gained a dedicated and passionate follower in Annie Kenney, a former mill girl, one of eleven children from a working class Yorkshire family, who became a close friend of the Pankhursts and an invaluable addition to the staff of the new Union.

Annie was appointed as a full-time official of the WSPU in London and, together with her sister Jessie, began to recruit more working class members.

In 1905 the WSPU persuaded John Bamford Slack, Liberal Member of Parliament for St. Albans, to introduce a Women's Suffrage Bill but MPs who were opposed to the advancement of women executed a filibuster by deliberately extending the debate until it was talked out. Mrs. Pankhurst and the officers of the WSPU were understandably incensed by such a discreditable and underhand tactic which, in the event, proved to be the catalyst for a hardening in their policy. From hereon the Union would oppose any person, party or manifesto which did not include support for women's suffrage. It also marked the start of serious civil disobedience and militant action.

Frederick and Emmeline Pethick-Lawrence, important supporters of the WSPU and founders of the paper *'Votes for Women'*.

In 1906 Annie Kenney had met Mrs. Emmeline Pethick-Lawrence a very influential socialist who had been engaged in charitable work and who, together with her husband Frederick, owned the left-wing evening newspaper *'The Echo'*. Mrs. Pethick-Lawrence was so impressed with the dedication of this young woman that she decided to become a member of the WSPU and within a very short space of time had become one of its most important officers. She was appointed as Treasurer and also demonstrated a great flair for publicity which she regularly used to the advantage of the WSPU.

Frederick Pethick-Lawrence, a wealthy business man, was also a strong believer in women's rights and with his wife took an interest in the Union's business. In 1907 they had started the first of the suffrage periodicals – *'Votes for Women'* with a cover price of one penny. The Pethwick-Lawrences also made their large house in Lincoln's Inn available to the WSPU as their headquarters.

So this was the WSPU whose breakfast meeting Sarah Benett had attended in January 1907. It was an organisation whose slogan 'Deeds not Words' had already been proven on several occasions with acts of civil disobedience and disruptive behaviour which had resulted in arrests and prison sentences. It was a group of women which had been derisively called 'Suffragettes' by the *'Daily Mail'* but had adopted this new word, which would soon be used as the generic term for all militant suffragists, with pride and delight. This seemed to be the sort of organisation Sarah had been looking for.

> *"I returned to my home in the Potteries and thought things over and I determined to swell the number of those who had adopted a new and, as it seemed to me absolutely necessary, plan for calling attention to outworn conventions and the anomalous position of women in (so called) modern civilizations.*
>
> *"I wrote to Clements Inn that, should my services be required, I should be prepared to take part in a deputation, and if this led to imprisonment I should not mind."* [2]

Sarah Benett, at the age of 57, was about to become a Suffragette.

2. Early Years

2 Chester Terrace, Marylebone, London.
14th November 1850

At four o'clock in the morning of Thursday 14th November 1850, Barbara Sarah Benett (née Waring) gave birth to a daughter at their Marylebone home in an exclusive area of London next to Regent's Park. It was a relatively easy birth as it was Barbara's seventh child and she was familiar with the procedures and knew exactly what to expect. On Sunday 22nd December the infant was baptised at the Church of the Holy Trinity, in Marylebone Road, and was christened Sarah.

Sarah's father, William Morgan Benett, was a successful barrister and his London house reflected his elevated social position. Chester Terrace, one of the most magnificent regency terraces in London, had been designed by John Nash and built by James Burton in 1825. There were forty-two houses in the unbroken terrace which was marked at either end by an impressive corinthian arch.

William and Sarah had been married in Penrith, Cumberland on 17th April 1843. The wedding was from the home of Barbara's sister, Annie, who was married to a Dr. Nicholson, and the following month the couple

had travelled to Southsea to spend a couple of days with Barbara's sister Fanny and her husband Frank Waring. Since then they had lived all their married lives in London. Although William had been

Chester Terrace, Regent's Park. No.2 is on the left hand side nearest the arch.

MIKE FAHERTY

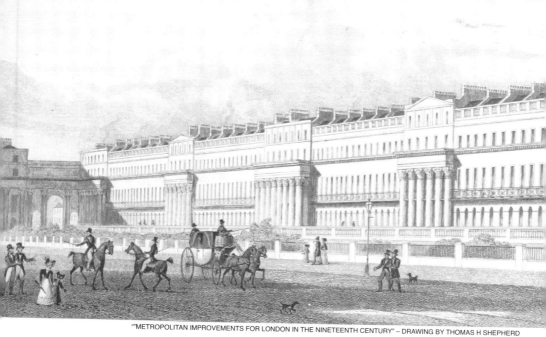

Chester Terrace, Regent's Park c.1850

born in Donhead St. Mary, Wiltshire, and Barbara in Tiverton, Devon, their family roots were in Lyme Regis, a small coastal town on the Devon/Dorset border. Both came from naval families: William's father, Charles Cowper Benett, had retired from the Royal Navy as a commander and had taken an active part in the affairs of Lyme Regis having been elected mayor three times. It was the practice of the day to bump long-retired naval officers up the promotion scale to create vacancies for serving officers lower down and he was thus promoted to captain in 1851. Barbara's father, Henry Waring, also retired from the Royal Navy in the rank of commander and never rose higher although he was known locally by the courtesy title of 'Captain'. A Waring uncle of Barbara's was Town Clerk of Lyme and both families were well established in the social hierarchy of the area and prominently placed in civic matters.

With William's growing reputation at the bar in London, and enjoying a very comfortable income, he and Barbara led the lives of a typical prosperous, professional, Victorian middle-class family. In 1844, the year after their marriage, their first child was born, a son, whom they christened William Charles after his father and paternal grandfather. Then in 1845 a daughter, Margaret Waring, and in 1846 Sarah Barbara. Mary Jane followed in 1847, Etheldred Fanny in 1848, Ann Burlton in 1849 and Sarah in 1850.

With seven children, Barbara employed two nursemaids, a senior aged 45 and her 19 year-old assistant. In addition to the nursemaids, there were three living-in servants – a cook, a housemaid and a 15 year-old page. Their neighbours in Chester Terrace were, in the main, prosperous merchants and successful professional people like themselves.

On Sundays William and Barbara, with whichever of the children were considered old enough, attended matins at the Holy Trinity Church in nearby Marylebone Road. This impressive building, where Sarah and her siblings were also christened, was one of the 'Waterloo Churches' built in 1828 by Sir John Sloane out of a fund of £1 million put aside by the government to celebrate the defeat of Bonaparte.

In 1852 Barbara gave birth to her second son, John Burlton, and another in 1854, the last of her nine children, who was christened Newton Burlton after Sir Isaac Newton who was a distant forbear.

Every year at the end of July, the family would move out of London for an 8-10 week holiday in Lyme Regis. If William was in the middle of a

PUBLIC DOMAIN – HASSOCKS 5489

Holy Trinity Church, Marylebone, one of the 'Waterloo Churches'.

case, he would join them later. In 1855 Barbara recorded in her diary:

> " *On 28th July went with the usual party to Lyme where we stayed with Capt. Benett until 5th October. Nothing could be pleasanter than this visit. The children took turns in riding with Capt. B. and bathed regularly all the time. William joined us in August.* " [3]

Captain Benett's house in Lyme, St. Andrew's, stood behind and above the town with splendid views across Lyme Bay to the English Channel. After the confinement of city life, the children enjoyed the freedom of a large garden, country life and the joy of sea bathing from the famous Cobb immortalised by Jane Austen as the place where Louisa Musgrove had her near-fatal fall in *'Persuasion'*.

In 1856, when Sarah was six, the health of two of her siblings was giving cause for concern. Ann, who was one year older than Sarah, had been experiencing fits, which did not seem to be improving, then Newton, the youngest caught measles very severely. His mother wrote:

> *"My little Newton caught the measles and was so ill that I thought he would never get better or, at any rate, that he would be blind. However, Captain Benett came to us and, seeing how ill he was, asked me to send him to Lyme, which I did."* [3]

The sea air helped the child to recover but the following year he stayed in London when the family went on their 10-week holiday to Lyme and, on their return, found him ill again:

> *"When we got home we found that our poor Newton had [a] lumbar abscess. Tried mesmerism for him and Annie but with no success except that he was in a mesmeric sleep when the abscess was opened and did not feel it."* [3]

In 1860, when Sarah was 10, her father was appointed a Master of the Court

The Court of Common Pleas sitting in Westminster Hall c.1822

of Common Pleas. This ancient part of the English judiciary, established in the 12th century, and authorised in the 'Magna Carta' to sit in Westminster Hall, dealt with common law cases where citizen fought citizen and the Crown was not involved.

With nine children in the house, No. 2 Chester Terrace was anything but quiet. A tutor, Miss Jones, came in daily to school the children; she was replaced later in the year by a Miss Barclay who, it appears, was equally demanding. One of the most lively of the children was Sarah Barbara who was five years older than Sarah and clearly a child of some spirit! On Tuesday 20th March she recorded in her diary:

> *"I dawdled over my dressing and was late for breakfast this morning so got sent up with a slice of dry bread which, however, I toasted and buttered upstairs. Lessons were pretty well. I don't like German, Latin is my best today. I shall be very glad when Miss Jones goes and we go to college for everything."* [4]

Rebel with a Cause

The next day Sarah Barbara and Margaret were confirmed by the Bishop of Carlisle for which they wore their lilac and white dresses and white caps. After the evening celebrations they had a scare on their way home:

> *"On our way home a man said to us 'Fine evening for your walk young ladies'. He followed us, or rather walked beside us all up Portland Place when we got separated, but he met us at the top of Albany Street. He frightened me horridly."* (4)

Sarah Barbara was continually being scolded for bad behaviour and poor performance in her lessons but she was not alone in her transgressions: on 9th April she recorded that all the children had been late down for breakfast and that Sarah and Etheldred had been whipped. As with all children, the absence of parents was an opportunity to kick over the traces. On 28th April she wrote:

> *"Mama is not very well today and we went to church without her. We behaved dreadfully in church for there was a young man there exactly like Apollo and I looked at him all the time, and they sang the hymn tune to which Willie [her brother] sings all kinds of absurd poetry and we couldn't help laughing."* (4)

Sarah Barbara's behaviour did not improve and she provided a very bad example to Sarah and her other younger sisters, perhaps planting the seeds of later rebellious behaviour. In July 1860 she recorded:

> *"On Friday after dinner I was playing and laughing with Mama when Etheldred came up and interfered and began to quarrel with me and then slapped me in the face and then I went into a tremendous passion and hit Ethel. Mama told me to go out of the room and I refused (Ethel says she hit me by accident but I don't see very well how she could do that) so then Mama and E. went out and locked me in after her so I*

said I would go out over the balustrades and come in at Papa's window. Mama said if I did I should be locked up in my own room for a week and I said I didn't care for I should if she didn't let me out so then she let me out but I was very impertinent afterwards. I'm sure I don't know what I said but Mama made me stay in the nursery all the afternoon, or at least told me to . . ." [4]

With the increased social status which her husband's new appointment gave her, Barbara's enjoyment of the annual holiday in Lyme began to be somewhat marred by the prospect of her children's London refinement being corrupted by the more provincial manners of Lyme!

"Early in August we all went to Lyme where I spent a very unhappy two months tormented by seeing all my children get into Lyme society and Lyme ways." [3]

This danger was certainly not recognised by the children who enjoyed themselves every bit as much as usual. Sarah Barbara was known as 'Barbara' to avoid confusion with her younger sister Sarah, but we shall continue to call her Sarah Barbara to avoid confusion with her mother!

Aged 15, Sarah Barbara, as usual, took Sarah, aged 10, under her wing and the summer was spent in a glorious round of sunny days when the children would bathe off the Cobb, ride on ponies, take long walks along the coast and visit friends and relations. However, there were clouds on the horizon and in October William and Barbara were shocked to learn that Captain Benett, aged 71, was to marry a Miss Orchard, a woman young enough to be his grand-daughter. They spent the remainder of the year:

". . . much troubled by this unfortunate affair." [3]

In February 1861, Captain Benett was married, to the distress of his family, and William and Barbara felt it would not be possible for them to continue their holidays in Lyme under these circumstances.

St. Andrew's, Lyme Regis.

"We can hardly expect to see them or the poor old place again and I think William and I are equally grieved." [3]

They also considered it necessary to bring the two delicate children, Annie and Newton, back to London from Lyme where they had both been living for the sake of their health, with Maria, the wife of an old and well-loved retainer. However:

" . . . after six weeks [we] found them so much worse and so difficult to manage in the house with so many, that we took a lodging for them at Hampstead." [3]

The schism in the family due to Captain Benett's marriage was to last another two years until May 1863 when the death from consumption of William's brother, Philip Benett, aged 28, took him to Lyme for the funeral and a reconciliation with his father.

In the same month, to her parents' great sorrow, Sarah's sister Annie died. Her fits, which had shown some improvement while she was living at Lyme, had deteriorated again. It is probable that she was epileptic. Her brother Newton, who was in the care of the same nurse as Annie in Hampstead, developed a further abscess on his spine and was in continual pain. The other children visited him regularly, either walking or by omnibus, but found the poor child's condition very distressing. He was to become a permanent hunchback.

And so Sarah's teenage years progressed – shopping in the West End, church services at Holy Trinity, visits to Newton, trips to the Park to watch the militia drilling, regular summer holidays in Lyme and long walks around London until she knew the thoroughfares of Central London intimately – an asset which would prove to be of much use to her in later years.

The first of the sisters to be married was Sarah Barbara. On 29th January 1868, at Holy Trinity, Marylebone Road, she married James Henry Allen, a junior partner in a firm of rope and cable manufacturers. The couple moved to Eliot Park, Lewisham in south-east London where they lived, in appropriate style for a rising young businessman, in a large, semi-detached house with four servants. The following January Sarah's first niece was born, Etheldred Margaret Allen, and in 1870 her first nephew, William Jeffreys Benett Allen.

On 13th June 1872 Sarah's second sister, Mary Jane, married Albert Reginald Graves, a Harrow and Cambridge educated barrister who was a Wiltshire magistrate and a captain in the Wiltshire Militia. He was a man of considerable substance having inherited the Charlton Estate in the village of Ludwell near Shaftesbury with 1,266 acres of land and five large farms. He also owned Delapre House in Bridport which had been built in the early 19th century as an Officers' Mess for a cavalry regiment stationed in Bridport as part of the coastal reinforcements to counter the threat of Bonaparte. After Waterloo it had been sold as a private house.

The couple alternated between their two homes and in 1873 Mary Jane gave birth to Mary Kate Graves and the following year to Reginald Burlton Graves. Sarah Barbara, meanwhile, had given birth to twins in 1872 – Constance Augusta Burlton and Arthur Henry Burlton Allen. Katherine Barbara, the last of their children, was to follow in 1875.

Fritham House, Bramshaw, which today is the New Forest Nursing Home.

By now the household at Chester Terrace was considerably reduced; Sarah's younger brother John had left home and was a midshipman in the Royal Navy; two daughters were married and William Benett had retired from the bar and had bought a house at Fritham in the New Forest where he had moved and, with a housekeeper, cook, coachman and outdoor team was getting the place in good order before his family joined him.

As a retired barrister of some note, William Benett took an active part in local affairs and, together with members of the other prominent families in Hampshire, supported and attended all the local events such as the Bramshaw and Nomansland Cottage Garden Show of which he became a patron. However, in 1870 he was elected to a position which would be of particular interest to Sarah and which would be instrumental in developing her views on, and ambitions for, society.

Workhouses had existed in Britain since the 17th century their purpose being to provide accommodation and gainful employment for destitute families and individuals as well as temporary shelter and corrective treatment for vagrants and drunks. Before their introduction, poor relief had been provided by the Parish with 'outpayments' which could comprise money, food or clothing, being made to the claimants in their own homes. By the early 19th century the cost of poor relief was becoming unacceptable and many thought the system was being abused by able-bodied people who were perfectly capable of obtaining normal employment. In 1832 the Government set up a Royal Commission to examine the problem.

The result of this was the *Poor Law Amendment Act 1834*, a refinement of previous legislation, which effectively put an end to 'outpayments' for

41

The New Forest Union Workhouse at Ashurst which conformed to the standard 'Union' star-shaped design giving three wings with segregated exercise areas between them.

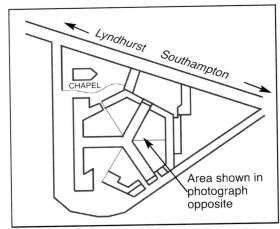

CHAPEL

Lyndhurst

Southampton

Area shown in photograph opposite

able-bodied people and decreed that a 'Poor Law Union' should be established to serve every parish in England and Wales. Each Union was to be governed by an elected Board of Guardians and in the years that followed hundreds of Union Workhouses were built many of which conformed to the standard 'Union' star-shaped design. This provided three radial wings at 120 degrees to each other to house male, female and infirm inmates with exercise areas between the wings each radially bisected by a wooden fence. The wings and the exercise areas were strictly segregated.

In 1835, in prompt implementation of the Act, the New Forest Poor Law Union had been inaugurated to provide and oversee workhouses in the New Forest. The Union was to be governed by a Board of 17 elected Guardians representing the nine constituent parishes. In 1870 William Benett was elected as Guardian for Bramshaw and was to be re-elected every year that he remained at Fritham House. Up until then, Sarah had lived the life of a child brought up in an affluent upper-middle class family. Now, taking an immediate interest in her father's connection with the workhouse, she was to see, for the first time, the wretchedness of poverty and ill health in people who had no money and no recourse to assistance from friends or relations. She sought every opportunity to accompany her father on his weekly visits to the workhouse at Ashurst and became increasingly sympathetic towards the plight of its inmates and increasingly determined to find ways of helping such people towards better lives.

The New Forest Union Workhouse, today the Ashurst Hospital, showing two of the radial wings and the exercise area between them.

Their lives were harsh. Rising at 6 am they had breakfast consisting of bread and gruel at 6.30 before starting work at 7. They worked until 12 noon when there was a one-hour break for dinner, which was their main meal of the day and generally comprised a strictly calculated allowance of boiled meat and potatoes. The water in which the meat had been boiled was made into a thin soup by the addition of a few potatoes, turnips and barley which was served to the inmates at supper after their 1pm to 6 pm work period. Between 7 and 8 pm they had one hour of free time before 'lights out' at 8 pm. Minor concessions were made for the infirm.

Women's work consisted mainly of laundry, cleaning, sewing and helping in the kitchen. If a man was fortunate enough to have a trade such as carpenter or plumber, he would be employed in maintenance of the buildings. Unskilled men would peel potatoes and tend the grounds and were often put to the traditional tasks of oakum picking, to provide caulking for naval ships, stone breaking, for road making, and bone crushing for agricultural fertiliser.

The Workhouse Chapel at Ashurst.

Prayers were held daily and inmates were required to attend church twice on Sundays. Anyone who failed to attend would be punished with the loss of their next meal. In many workhouses services were held in the dining hall but Ashurst was one of those fortunate enough to have their own consecrated chapel which can still be seen today. Later in her career, Sarah would have the opportunity to compare the harshly ordered regime of the workhouse with that of prison which, in many ways she was to find, offered its residents greater indulgence and liberality.

Sarah's first active project was the formation of a co-operative store. The seeds of the co-operative movement had been sown by Robert Owen, a Welsh social reformer, in the 1820s and formation of the first co-operative societies, all in the North of England, began in the 1840s. Their purpose was to establish retail stores and manufacturing units to provide working families with good value products, and later services, and to free them from the tyranny of the 'Company Stores' which were operated by ruthless employers to lock their employees into continued service through debt and dependence. In the 1870s, workers from the North of England, migrating south to work in Portsmouth Dockyard, brought the co-operative message with them and in 1873 the first southern co-op shop was opened in Portsmouth and from here the concept was to spread throughout the South of England.

Though no record of Sarah's venture remains, it was probably in the village of Bramshaw, some two miles east of Fritham House, and might well have been started with some of her father's employees. In an interview in 1910 she said:

"My first serious effort to help things along was to start a co-operative society in the little village in the New Forest where the greater part of my youth was spent. I had a firm belief in those days that co-operation and trades unionism were going to regenerate society, so I got together a committee of working men, and acted as their secretary for eleven years." [5]

They must have been tough years as many manufacturers and distributors, anxious to retain the goodwill of the powerful employers and the tradesmen whose business was under threat, refused to supply the new co-operatives. Until the formation of the Women's Co-operative Guild (WCG) in 1883, women were barred from holding executive positions within the movement which may account for the fact that Sarah, who was probably the best educated and most capable person in her group, could only fill the lowly post of secretary to the Committee.

The outdoor staff at Fritham House, possibly the founder members of Sarah's first co-operative.

In 1877 Captain Benett died. He was not a rich man leaving less than £800 to his surviving son William who was his sole executor. Though he had inherited St. Andrews, the captain's house in Lyme Regis, William continued living at Fritham for the time being where he was well settled and deeply involved in local affairs.

In the same year, 1877, Sarah's sister Etheldred was married at Kennington, Surrey, to Charles James Connell, of the Bengal Civil Service and the elder son of James Connell, Vicar of Hammersmith. She travelled out to India with him and died the following year after giving birth to a son, Islay Benett Campbell Connell, on 14th November. The infant had been baptised twelve days later and was then sent back to England into the care of his mother's family who, fearing he may not have been baptised in India, had the service undertaken again at Holy Trinity, Marylebone in June 1879. Sadly, the poor motherless infant, weakened by a difficult birth and a long sea voyage, died at Fritham House later in the year before he had reached his first birthday.

Meanwhile, Sarah's younger brother John, now Lieutenant RN serving in HMS *Boadicea*, had been sent into the Naval Brigade attached to the British Force fighting King Cetshwayo in the Zulu War. In 1879 John was

The Battle of Gingindhlovo in which Sarah's brother John took part.

BUZZ SOUTH AFRCA

present at the Battle of Gingindhlovo as part of a column sent to relieve a small detachment at Eshowe which was under siege by the Zulus. In the early morning of 2nd April John and his men had witnessed the terrifying sight of a Zulu impi advancing on three sides of the British force in the traditional buffalo formation; but the relief column was equipped with Gatling guns which wrought havoc among the brave Zulu warriors who were able to inflict very little damage on the British. Only one Zulu reached the British line, a ten year-old boy who was spared the fate of his fellows in view of his age. The boy was taken by the sailors back on board HMS *Boadicea* where he became the ship's mascot.

However, John had become seriously ill during his time in Africa and was invalided back to England in November 1879. His condition did not improve and he died the following year in the Royal Naval Hospital Haslar, at Gosport. Mary Jane's husband, Reginald Graves, died in the same year leaving her a widow at the age of 34 with two young children. However, her husband had left them well provided for.

Sarah now had just one unmarried sister remaining – Margaret Waring Benett who, in July 1881, was married from Fritham House to Arthur Knatchbull Connell, an Oxford graduate who was the younger brother of Charles Connell who had married poor Etheldred four years earlier.

By 1881 Sarah Barbara and her husband James Allen had taken over the London house in Chester Terrace where they lived with their two children.

Etheldred and William. With a vast merchant fleet and the Royal Navy engaged in colonial and policing operations throughout the world, the demand for ropes and cable was heavy and James's business was thriving to the extent that he could now afford to live in one of the smartest parts of London with six servants including a ladies' maid for Sarah Barbara. He also

Margaret Waring Connell (née Benett) Sarah's oldest sister.

Barbara Waring Benett (née Waring) at Fritham House with seven of her grandchildren, five Allens and two Graves's c.1889.

generously allowed their house to serve as the London base for all visiting relatives; Sarah spent much time there and Mary Jane, after the loss of her husband, came for an extended stay with her two children, Mary and Reginald, while her late husband's affairs were being settled and she was looking for a smaller and more manageable house to buy.

It would seem that William Morgan Benett remained at Fritham House for as long as he could. The house and grounds were beautiful and much loved by all the family. One of his granddaughters later wrote:

> " . . . as children we always used to go there for our holidays and there we found a complete and glorious paradise on earth." [6]

However, towards the end of the 1880s his wife Barbara's health began to deteriorate and William decided to move to her childhood home town, Lyme Regis, where she would feel most at home and could return to the care of her well regarded and trusted physician, a Dr. Carey of Little Park. She appears to have been suffering from dementia, her behaviour became very erratic and she was increasingly difficult to handle. In the 1891 census she was recorded as an 'imbecile' which is how dementia sufferers were categorised at the time

By 1890 William's mental health was also suffering and to make matters worse they had each developed an apparent dislike for the other and would engage in terrible rows if they should meet in house or garden. In the Victorian tradition, Sarah's duty, as the only remaining unmarried daughter, was to stay at home and look after her parents which, towards the end, was not an enviable task.

Newton, now permanently in a wheelchair with a little donkey to pull him up the steep hills in Lyme Regis, was living in his parents' house but hated to be left alone in the house with them as he could not handle their scenes. He had set up a studio for himself in the town to which he could escape when things became difficult. Despite his disability, Newton was gaining a

Newton Benett *(left)* **with his cousin Henry Waring at Lyme Regis.**

LYME REGIS MUSEUM

reputation for watercolours of forest scenes and landscapes and his paintings still change hands today for four-figure sums.

Constance Allen, Sarah Barbara's second daughter, recorded some of the difficulties she had with her grandparents in her diary:

> ". . . *Grandma is trying, too, and wearying when she is fractious which she very often is, poor old thing . . . [Grandpapa] has been very seedy lately and weeps and laments a good deal, especially at meal times – the noise he makes sometimes is truly appalling."* [6]

On 9th October 1891 she wrote:

> *"Grandpapa has been very ill indeed and quite off his head – much madder than Grandmama . . . when I came back Ethel was very nervous as Gran'pa was wandering about, not knowing in the least where he was going, or what he was doing or saying, and swearing awfully if he came across Gran'ma in the passage. Elizabeth went for Dr. Bangay at once and he came, then again at midnight and again at 7 am in the morning."* [6]

Four days later, when they got back from church:

> *"We found that Gran'ma had locked herself in the drawing-room and couldn't unlock it again; we sent the boy down in a tremendous hurry for the carpenter and after a long struggle he succeeded in forcing the lock . . . Altogether, between these two old people, we have a very exciting time of it, first one then the other, we're never dull."* [6]

Twelve days later on 25th October 1891, William Morgan Benett died peacefully in his sleep and was buried quietly at Uplyme where he had worshipped whenever he was in Lyme Regis.

Rebel with a Cause

During these years at Lyme Sarah had acquired considerable experience in looking after elderly people but had also developed a special interest in the younger members of the family. She regularly accompanied them on outings and to social events and her strength of character and determination were evidently becoming familiar to her, not always appreciative, nieces and nephews. She would make them walk for distances they would never have themselves contemplated, swam strongly and played tennis regularly and her fearless, if reckless, driving filled them with terror! Constance wrote:

> "I went with Aunt Sarah to call on Lady Tulloch; we went in the dog-cart so I was in a horrid fright the whole time, especially coming back when Belle was very lively, for I place no confidence whatever in Aunt Sarah's driving and the way she goes down some of those steep hills is awfully alarming: she holds the reins quite slack and lets Belle fly down at the top of her speed which is extremely rapid. I don't like it at all."
> (6)

She also developed their fortitude and endurance in other ways; Constance recorded an occasion when they had attended an evening entertainment:

> "It was only Aunt Sarah, Ethel and I who went, Aunt Margaret and Uncle Willie wouldn't come. It was a very wild night and raining when we got out but Aunt Sarah insisted on our walking home instead of waiting for the fly, which was a mad thing to do as we were in evening dress and had nothing on our heads. Luckily neither we nor our dresses are the worse for it." (6)

As well as physical fitness, Sarah was also developing a keen interest in education and, with the help of Constance and Etheldred, arranged a programme of 'Oxford Extension Lectures' for the winter months of 1892 and, together, they drummed up sufficient people to attend.

Sarah loved animals and was Secretary of the local Society for the Prevention of Cruelty to Animals.

Though she was living the life of a lady and was mixing in the higher social circles of Devon and Dorset, Sarah's interest in and concern for the poor and disadvantaged was unabated. She had gained some experience of their problems at the New Forest Workhouse, and with her co-operative venture in Bramshaw. Her sense of duty would not permit her to walk out on her elderly mother but she was increasingly discontent with the meaningless life she was leading and yearned for the opportunity to do something really worthwhile. She read a lot and attended political meetings and lectures whenever she could, sometimes taking with her a reluctant niece. She also had a great love of animals and served as Secretary of the local 'Society for the Prevention of Cruelty to Animals' (SPCA).

On 18th January 1894 Sarah's mother died. She was buried with her husband in the churchyard at Uplyme. William Benett had died a wealthy man with his estate valued at £55,916. 8s. 4d. Shortly before his death he had sold Fritham to a Mr. Bradburne for £3,000. This, the house in Lyme Regis and the bulk of the balance of his estate, he left to his eldest son William. However, he made generous bequests to all his other children and made special provision for the two unmarried ones, Sarah and Newton. Sarah shared in a number of minor bequests with her siblings and, most importantly, received from her father an income for life of about £600 pa

The grave of Sarah's parents in Uplyme Churchyard (with her maternal grandfather's rank incorrectly engraved as "Captain RN")

LYME REGIS MUSEUM

from the investment of £4,000 in 15% consols. Trustees of the capital were her brothers-in-law James Allen and Arthur Connell who were also executors of William's Will.

Interestingly, his bequest of £2,500 in shares to his daughter Margaret Connell was made, as was the normal practice of the time, to the Trustees of her Marriage Settlement which would have given her husband access to the money. However, in a codicil made the year before his death he revoked this bequest in favour of:

> ". . . *a legacy of £2,500 sterling for her own absolute use and benefit.*" [7]

Times, it seems, were beginning to change and the injustice of married women having no control over their own money was starting to be recognised at least in some quarters.

Sarah was now, at last, independent and could decide where she wanted to live and, at the age of 44, what course the rest of her life was to take. Her leanings had become increasingly left-wing over the years and her sympathies and interest lay with the emerging Labour Party, the trades unions and the co-operatives which she saw as the best way of improving the lot of hard-pressed working families, the section of society she was determined to serve.

She could now live anywhere in the country she pleased and, after much deliberation, she decided to go to an area which was highly industrialised and notoriously disadvantaged in terms of health, education and standards of living. After the burial of her mother and the settlement of her parents' affairs, Sarah packed up her few belongings and moved to the Staffordshire Potteries in the West Midlands.

3. The Potteries

Burslem, Staffordshire, 1894

The 'Five Towns' of the Potteries, immortalised by Arnold Bennett in his *'Clayhanger'* novels, should actually have been 'Six Towns' but Bennett, it is said, preferred the sound of 'Five Towns' to 'Six Towns" and, for no better reason, the sixth town was expunged from his stories. The six towns were, Tunstall, Burslem, Hanley, Stoke-upon-Trent, Fenton and Longton which today have merged into each other and form districts of the city of Stoke-on-Trent.

The concentration of pottery manufacturers in North Staffordshire originated with the abundance of the local red clay which, as far back as mediaeval times, was made into coarse earthenware pots which were sold in local markets. At that time potting was a cottage industry undertaken seasonally by farmers who, as demand increased, built separate premises on their land with their own kilns and clay pits. Soon, the famous bottle-shaped kilns began appearing on farms throughout the area and the earthenware Staffordshire butter pots became available throughout the Midlands.

By the early18th century the rural potters had mostly moved into what became the six towns with Burslem as the hub of the new industry. Skilled craftsmen began to emerge and pass their skills on to their sons and others; famous names such as Wedgwood established potbanks, as factories were called, and outside manufacturers began to move into the area to take advantage of the local materials and skills. Investment in the industry increased and serious attempts were made to move from the crude earthenware products to the fine white ceramics which were in growing demand. At the time, these could only be obtained from China and later from the great continental producers such as Meissen and Sèvres who enjoyed royal patronage and could therefore engage in greater research and development than could the self-supporting Staffordshire industry.

The breakthrough came in 1720 when John Astbury discovered that the coveted white china could be produced by the addition of finely ground and graded flint to the local clay. The flint had to come from Cornwall but to balance the cost of this, most of the potbanks were converting to more efficient coal firing so they could take advantage of the vast local coalfields which covered 100 square miles. From thereon a huge nationwide market began to develop and the potbanks of the six towns advanced their skills and production methods until they were manufacturing fine ceramics which could compete with goods from Europe and China. Names which would become household words such as Wedgwood, Doulton, Minton and Twyford became the major employers in the Potteries.

Social conditions, however, did not advance at the same rate as industrial innovation. Workers' housing, hastily built and without sound planning for sanitation, sprang up outside the potbank gates. Outbreaks of cholera were not unusual and, with the whole area enveloped in smoke from the bottle kiln chimneys, the quality of air was appalling; it was said that a fine day in the Potteries was when you could see the other side of the street.

New techniques in the industry brought with them new occupational hazards to workers' health. Silicosis, or 'Potters' Rot' as it was known in Staffordshire, was widespread. It was caused by inhalation of the flint dust which was added to the local clay for whiteware and caused damage to the lungs which resulted in early death. The other principal killer was lead poisoning; glazed pottery required lead which, despite ongoing efforts to develop a leadless glaze, continued to kill the workers who came in contact with it well into the 20th century.

Industrial disease, overcrowding and poor sanitation were exacerbated by a culture of heavy drinking – a health hazard in itself but one which, more importantly, eroded the already meagre wage packets leaving wives and children short of essential food and clothing. Conditions in the workplace were usually no better. As a result of the 1842 *Factories Act Extension*, the Potteries received their first factories inspector, a Dr. Robert Baker who, despite constant opposition from the potbank owners and managers, was to play a major part in the gradual reform of safety, disease and hygiene in the industry.

A view of Longton in the Potteries c.1895

When he arrived in the Potteries in 1858 Dr. Baker found:

> " *The most wretched hole imaginable . . . most of the outside steps were without handrails and were thus exceedingly dangerous when used at night. The work rooms were hot and comfortless and had not been whitewashed for years. On asking to see the privies here I found one horrible place for all the workers, without any doors, in front of a place of work constantly in use, with the people passing up and down in sight of it in every direction; no accommodation whatever for females.*" [8]

The understandable disaffection of the workers had come to a head with strikes in the 1820s and 30s but in 1842 events had taken place in the Potteries which were to be major factors in the introduction of trades unions in Staffordshire and the establishment of strike action as the last resort in labour disputes. The troubles in 1842 started with the Staffordshire coal miners who were threatened with a reduction of a shilling a day in their wages without the employers having given them the statutory notice. This was the start of the 1842 General Strike which soon spread throughout the area.

In the middle of this, the pottery workers in Burslem and Hanley gave vent to their real grievances in what became know as the 'Pottery Riots'. They were actively supported by the Chartists, a working class movement for long overdue electoral reform. An observer wrote that the rioters:

> "... *broke open the Police Office at Hanley, also a print-works, also a principle pawnbroker's shop there, and the house of the tax collector; proceeded to Stoke, demolished the windows of that Post Office, and afterwards those of Fenton and Longton.*
>
> "*The rectory-house at the latter place was the especial object of their fury; it was gutted and set fire to, though the fire was extinguished before it destroyed the premises. The house of Mr. Mason at Heron Cross, that of Mr. Allen of Great Fenton, and that of Mr. Rose, the police magistrate at Penkhull, were in like manner visited and treated by parties of marauders, who, returning to Hanley in the evening, were again lectured, and commended by Cooper [the Chartist representative] for what they had done, though he reproved them for their drunkenness, as being likely to expose them to detection. Terror and consternation spread around, and many families left home for security. The scenes of the night were expected to surpass the atrocities of the day, and so they did.*
>
> "*Religion and justice must be exhibited as public victims on the altar of Chartist divinity. Accordingly the parsonage of the Rev. R. E. Aitkens in Hanley, and Albion House in Shelton, the residences of William Parker, Esq., one of the county magistrates, were, with all their valuable furniture, burnt and*

destroyed. The offices of Earl Granville in Shelton shared the same fate. The morning of the 16th discovered their smoking ruins." [9]

The riots did not last long and swift retribution followed. A special assizes was convened to try the 274 rioters who had been arrested of which 54 were transported to Australia and 146 were imprisoned. At the beginning of September the *'Staffordshire Advertiser'* reported:

"Nothing has occurred during the week to excite any fear of there being a renewal of the alarming tumults which have recently convulsed the district. Whether this state of things results from the disaffected and violent seeing the folly and wickedness of their late conduct, or the committal to prison of so many of their associates, or whether it has been produced by the vigorous measures of a protective character which have been adopted throughout the districts and which comprise an effective watch and ward, both by night and day, is not easily determined. It is to be hoped, however, that the first of these causes has in some degree assisted in the restoration of tranquility." [10]

The positive achievements of the events of 1842 had been the establishment, later in the same year, of 'The Miners' Association of Great Britain and Ireland' and 'The United Branches of Operative Potters' two of the earliest, and much needed, trades unions for the protection of workers.

The General Strike had increased public awareness of the appalling conditions in the potbanks and this was furthered by the report of the Government Commissioner, Dr. Samuel Scriven, into the employment of children in factories. This revealed that hundreds of children under 13 were employed, a 10 year-old typically working from 7 am to 6 pm for a wage of two shillings a week. [11]

Over the next half century until Sarah Benett arrived in Burslem in 1894, improvements had been made in working conditions in the potbanks; many

**196 Waterloo Road, Burslem
(right hand end of terrace, corner
house) where Sarah Bennet lived from
1896 to 1906**

of the problems of safety and ventilation had been addressed but the industry had expanded significantly and these advances had often been negated by the huge increase in population and the problems of housing, sanitation and education which it brought. Much still needed to be done.

Following the death of her mother, Sarah moved to The Potteries in 1894 and took temporary lodgings for two years before finding and buying a suitable house in a terrace of quite up-market villas on Waterloo Road, one of the principal thoroughfares through the six towns.

Burslem must have been quite a shock to her after the quiet and pleasant seaside town from where she had come. It was known as 'The Mother Town of The Potteries' and by the early 18th century, 43 of the 52 potbanks in the Six Towns had been established in Burslem. It had the grandest Town Hall in Staffordshire and an impressive town centre but, despite its handsome public buildings, the overwhelming aspect of the town was the smut-blackened houses of the workers and the cloud of smoke from the kilns which hung over the whole area. Though Sarah was probably aware that there was a certain magnificence in the wealth that its smoky industries were creating, the hardship and poverty which existed in the back streets of the town were of more concern to her.

Arnold Bennett actually found some beauty in Burslem, or Bursley as he called it in his novels:

> *"In front, on a little hill in the vast valley, was spread out the Indian-red architecture of Bursley – tall chimneys and rounded ovens, schools, the new scarlet market, the grey tower of the old church, the high spire of the evangelical church, the low spire of the church of genuflexions, and the crimson chapels, and rows of little red buildings with amber chimney-pots, and the gold angel of the blackened town hall topping the whole. The sedate reddish browns and reds of the composition, all netted in flowing scarves of smoke, harmonised exquisitely with the chill blues of the chequered sky. Beauty was achieved, and none saw it."* [12]

So this was the town in which Sarah had elected to live and whose disadvantaged people she was determined to assist. Few records remain of her achievements during her twelve years in the Potteries, and she left no notes or memoirs of this period of her life other than to record her bitter disappointment at having failed to receive the support and recognition she felt she merited and which was necessary for her to make any real progress in the programmes of welfare and reform which she had set herself. What is certain is that she worked tirelessly and persistently to gain access to those bodies which influenced matters concerning the welfare of workers and their families.

These areas were: Co-operation, Trades Unionism and Education. Of the first, with her experience of setting up and running a co-operative store in Hampshire, she looked into the possibility of doing the same in her new home town. In an article in 1910 Sarah recorded:

> *"Then, after my mother died, I went to the Potteries district and made my home in Burslem. I hadn't been there long before I started another co-operative society in Hanley, which ran a general store, of which I was practical manager."* [5]

The first co-operative in the Potteries, according to the Co-operative Society records, was opened on 22nd February 1901, at 8 Newcastle Street, Burslem, by James Colclough, a Burslem potter, to be followed three days later by the opening of the Hanley Industrial Provident Co-operative Society, general merchants, at 43 York Street, Hanley. This was seven years after Sarah's arrival in Burslem and there is evidence of her involvement with the movement well before this date. It is probable, therefore, that the store to which she referred was an unofficial co-operative which might well have led the way to the later establishment of the officially-sponsored outlets. It is certain that her previous experience would have proved valuable to the founders, among whom was Fred Hayward, another son of a Burslem potter, who held many important positions in the movement in Staffordshire, and

Sir Frederick Hayward 1876-1944, one of the founders of the Co-operative movement in Staffordshire.

THE POTTERIES.ORG

The Old Town Hall in Burslem which today houses the 'Ceramica' Exhibition.

ANDREW WOODVINE

eventually nationally, and was elected as Lord Mayor of Stoke-on-Trent in 1926. Having held many senior appointments after a life of public service, he was knighted in 1931 and died in 1944.

It was not long after her arrival that Sarah, with her passionate desire to assist in the improvement of conditions for workers and their families, became involved in the local trades unions:

> *"I also attended constantly the meetings of a women potters'*
> *trade union, and it was during my association with that, that*
> *I investigated the terrible tragedies caused by lead poisoning.*
> *These led me to draft an appeal for help to the 'Daily*
> *Chronicle' and this was the beginning of the agitation against*
> *the reckless use of lead glaze, which has had many good*
> *results."* [5]

The *Factories and Workshops Bill,* introduced in 1891, had addressed measures for the protection of workers principally in the textiles industries.

A J Mundella .

THE REVIEW OF REVIEWS (1891) NEW YORK, LONDON

Trades union members from the Potteries had seen this as an opportunity to have the hazards of their own trades specifically included and started to lobby Parliament for an appropriate amendment. They had gained the support of two prominent and influential Members of Parliament – Sir Henry James and Mr. A J Mundella and an amendment had been duly added to extend protection to workers involved in 'dusty processes'.

From this Act, known at the time as 'The Potters' Charter for Health', stemmed all the remedial measures which would be gradually introduced over the next several years. Two years later in 1893, the Home Office, having declared the potting industry to involve processes *"Damaging to Health"*, had appointed a committee to:

> *"Make inquiry into the conditions under which the manufacture of pottery is carried on, with the object of diminishing any proved ill effects in the health of the work people engaged therein."*

An analysis of mortality among males aged over 14 in Stoke-on-Trent in the year 1890 had shown that 42% had died of pneumonia, 8% of pleurisy and 21% of pulmonary consumption. The committee had therefore concluded that:

> *"The inference is consequently unavoidable that potters suffer an excessive mortality in following their occupation and that the mineral dust they inhale is largely accountable for it."*

The committee had recommended that the Home Secretary should ratify the special rules they had previously proposed.

These rules, which included such measures as the installation of fans in some of the older premises, were hotly contested by many of the manufacturers on the grounds of impracticality though the reformers claimed it was simply that they were not prepared to spend the money.

However, as time went on, the majority of employers accepted the necessity of the new rules and the war against toxic dust made steady progress; but little had been achieved with regard to lead poisoning.

Sarah set about looking into the processes and areas of manufacture where workers were exposed to lead. She regularly attended meetings of the women potters' trade union and gained their trust and co-operation in her research. There were several areas in any potbank where workers were regularly exposed to lead but the most vulnerable occupation was that of the dippers and their assistants whose job was to plunge the finished ware into a bath in which the finely-ground glaze was suspended in water.

Inevitably, the suspension was splashed onto the dippers' clothing which then dried out and was inhaled and absorbed through the skin.

The principal family in the Potteries at that time was the immensely rich Sutherland-Leveson-Gowers, Dukes of Sutherland who, among several other titles, were also Marquesses of Stafford and Viscounts Trentham. Trentham was their Staffordshire seat in the Potteries. The Duchess Millicent was one of the great society hostesses of the time entertaining royalty and the cream of metropolitan society at her palatial home in London, Stafford House, and at Dunrobin Castle, ancient seat of the Earls

Millicent, Duchess of Sutherland
(*detail in black and white from the painting by John Singer Sarjent*)

MUSEO THYSSEN-BORNEMISZA, MADRID

Professor Thomas Edward Thorpe, Director of the Government Laboratory who headed the 1898 Inquiry into lead poisoning in pottery manufacture.

JOURNAL OF THE CHEMICAL SOCIETY

of Sutherland in the north of Scotland. However, she was also deeply concerned with the welfare of the workers in the Potteries which earned her the name 'Meddlesome Millie' with the manufacturers and she was satirised by Arnold Bennett in his Five Towns books as *'the countess with an interfering meddlesomeness which so frequently exasperates the Five Towns'*.

Sarah soon recognised the powerful influence for social reform which the Duchess could bring to bear upon government and worked closely with her in the campaign against lead poisoning. She is credited with having supplied the Duchess with much of the detail she had acquired from her researches and her trades union contacts. It was a strange liaison since, at the same time, Sarah was leading a protest against the Sutherland Estates concerning the closure of an alleged right-of-way in the Trentham grounds which, apparently, had infuriated the Duke and ended up in a civil action.

With the strength of the Duchess's sponsorship behind it, the campaign against lead glazes resulted, in 1898, in the commissioning of a government inquiry to establish just how necessary lead glaze was in pottery manufacture. The Home Secretary appointed two eminent authorities in the field to head the inquiry – Professor Thomas Edward Thorpe, Director of the Government Laboratory, and Dr. Thomas Oliver, a recognised expert in lead poisoning. Their Report to the Home Secretary stated:

> *"We have no doubt whatever that leadless glazes of sufficient brilliancy, covering power and durability, and adapted to all kinds of table, domestic and sanitary ware are now within the reach of the manufacturers."* [13]

While conceding that there were still some limited areas within the industry where the use of lead was essential, the Report advised that the greater part of the output from the potbanks could be produced using lead-free glazes. It also recommended that the use of raw lead should be absolutely prohibited, that young persons and women should be prohibited from working with lead and that male workers should be subject to regular and mandatory medical examinations.

Needless to say, this Report was greeted with fury by the manufacturers who hotly disputed the stage at which the development of leadless glazes had reached. However, fearing that a lack of co-operation from the industry might drive the Government into a sudden and arbitrary ban on lead, the manufacturers expressed their willingness to comply with the Report's recommendations but pleaded for time to effect the necessary changes. This the Government granted and by the summer of 1900 many enlightened manufacturers had introduced leadless glazes and the others had accepted the fact that the changeover was inevitable. In 1901 Duchess Millicent expressed the hope that:

> *". . . the via media be taken unquestioningly by the master and the workman of good intention; let them in mutual trust and confidence, even if stronger trade combinations are a necessity of the position, accept the inevitable and mould the inevitable to mutual profit and advancement. The Government has done much, the manufacturers may do more – not only in the letter of reform, but in the spirit thereof – by passing from the pettiness of recrimination and continual antagonism to reform, to a higher altitude where every advantage may be taken of scientific discovery and enlightened education and where, infused with a new energy and enthusiasm, they may make their trade not only one of the most beautiful, but in organisation one of the most perfect in the world."* [13]

Sarah Benett must be given due credit for the major part she played behind the scenes in this necessary crusade which, on balance, and in no small part due to the support of the Duchess of Sutherland, must be regarded as having been successful.

The third area to which Sarah devoted her time and energy during her period in the Potteries was education – a subject which had held considerable interest for her since her days in Fritham and Lyme Regis.

She served for a time as the Labour member, and the only female member, of the 'Burslem School Board' from where she hoped to influence education policy in the Potteries. However, her ideas were received with a degree of derision by the other, largely Conservative, members until the *1902 Education Act*:

> "... *took from women the right of election. After that they could only be co-opted and I was not co-opted.*" [2]

Sarah had high expectations of how a reformed attitude to education could lead, in time, to greatly improved standards of living for workers' families. She was appalled by the apparently ignorant and helpless state in which traditional education left the majority of its beneficiaries:

> "*The mass of people know little or nothing of the laws of health, even as to such things as washing, fresh air and regular hours. Think of the number of people one sees who don't seem to have a sensible thought in their heads. Think of their cooking and housekeeping, of the way they squander their money when they have any. Such people have no knowledge of life, or faith, or judgment, or self-restraint. What education have these had? Their minds are a blank, they don't think – they drift. Even of book-learning I doubt whether they remember more than a little reading or writing. They are sent rudderless into the world to sink or swim, and the money spent on their schooling might just as well have been thrown into the canal.*" [14]

Her concept of education was far broader than that which was practised at the time. She believed that critical thinking would ultimately be of more use to pupils than the basic skills acquired by ruthless rote tuition. Her beliefs were founded on classical precedents – Plato, Pestalozzi and even Dr. Edward Thring, the celebrated headmaster of Uppingham and founder of the 'Headmasters' Conference'.

However, her fellow Board Members tended to be hard-headed, self-made men who did not recognise themselves as the dysfunctional creatures described by this airy-fairy lady from the soft south of England. Traditional education had not held them back in achieving wealth and influence and they could see no reason to condemn or change existing practices. They were, in all probability, much relieved when the opportunity arose to rid themselves of this troublesome lady.

But Sarah would not give up that easily and continued to lobby for educational reform with every opportunity which presented itself. In 1900 she was invited by the Stoke Branch of the 'Women's Co-operative Guild' to deliver to its members a paper on her ideas for educational reform. This was later reprinted in three weekly parts in the *'Co-operative News'* and is reproduced in full at the end of this chapter.

In October 1907 Sarah stood for election to the Burslem Town Council believing that she enjoyed the support of the trades unions to which she had devoted so much of her time and energy; but their support was not forthcoming and she was not elected. This was a bitter disappointment to her as her name had become well known throughout the Potteries and she felt that she enjoyed the confidence of the potters' families for whom she could have achieved a great deal if she had been returned to office.

It was at this point that Sarah assessed her achievements during the eleven years she had been in the Potteries and concluded, rather despairingly, that they amounted to absolutely nothing. She had been rejected both by the authorities in the three areas in which she had attempted to bring change and, more ironically, by the people for whose interests she had been fighting. This she attributed to the fact that she was a woman and had come to believe that she would make no further progress during the remainder of her life so long as the opinions of women were held in such little regard.

When asked in 1910 what had induced her to forsake trade unionism and co-operation she replied:

> *"I should hardly say I have forsaken them, for I still keep in touch with some of them and make translations for their papers sometimes. But I found as years went on that the co-operative system was captured by people who were actuated by the worst spirit of commercialism, and the ideals of the pioneers of the movement were lost sight of; and that trade unionists, in many ways, held narrow and conservative views and were not real social reformers. But, after all, this is only another way of saying that they were tainted with the spirit of the age – a self-seeking, self-advertising materialism. And so I came to see that if one wants to give permanent help, one must endeavour to change the spirit of the age even more than the wrongs that it fosters. This can only be done by the bringing into every phase of life the woman's outlook and ideals. So, you see, I found, as the rest of you did, that all roads lead to votes for women."* [5]

And so it was that Sarah Benett decided to leave the Potteries and devote the remainder of her life to the fight for women's rights.

EDUCATION

A Paper Read by Miss Sarah Benett to the Stoke Branch
of the Women's Co-operative Guild in 1900

(Reprinted in three consecutive parts in the *"Co-operative News"*
September 1st, 8th and 15th, 1900.)

We must often feel very sad when we think what boys and girls are when they leave school. Some have bad homes, and those who have good parents do not always turn out well. The time spent in school has little influence for good on their lives. The mass of people know little or nothing of the laws of health, even as to such things as washing, fresh air and regular hours. Think of the number of people one sees who don't seem to have a sensible thought in their heads. Think of their cooking and housekeeping, of the way they squander their money when they have any. Such people have no knowledge of life, or faith, or judgment, or self-restraint. They listen to the self-interested advice of agents and travellers and let themselves be flattered into joining fraudulent societies, and then complain that people rob the poor. They will join a shop club, where they get about 12s. worth of things after they have paid £1; or they will drag on a life of perfect slavery to the little shop from which they get 'trust', obliged to take any trash at any price, or they will put into a 'Maxim' which costs them £1. 1s. in weekly payments because they have the excitement of receiving £1 all at once – and they generally waste it. Or they will go to the public-house when they get their wages, and live in misery all the rest of the week. What education have these had? Their minds are a blank, they don't think – they drift. Even of book-learning I doubt whether they remember more than a little reading or writing. They are sent rudderless into the world to sink or swim, and the money spent on their schooling might just as well have been thrown into the canal.

I hope to show you that it is not misplaced to address a guild of women on this subject. We are all, more or less, educators, and have an immense influence. We have to throw off centuries of intellectual slavery, and be as clever and independent in our judgments as nature meant us to be.

I wanted to say a little about the history of education, but there will not be time. I would have told you how it was that book learning came to be put in the place of education, and how much harm this has done and is doing. Instead, I will speak of two educationists whose thoughts ought to be familiar to us all, and then I will try to show you what I think our aims should be.

PLATO

Plato, who lived about 500 B.C. at Athens, wrote a good many books – one called *'The Republic'* which, like More's *'Utopia'*, is the picture of a model state, and he says a great deal about how the citizens should be educated.

One important part of teaching, he said, was talking and reasoning with young people. The teacher and pupils should take walks together and talk, and notice things. This he called 'dialectics'. The teacher asked questions and let the pupil express his thoughts freely, and then led him to see where he was mistaken. *'The Republic'* itself is a dialogue. In one passage a pupil says he thinks it is to a man's advantage to be thoroughly unjust, so long as he can evade the penalty of his crimes. The master answers:

> *"Figure the human soul as a man, a lion and a many-headed monster combined under a human form. My pupil Thrasymachus says it is expedient to be unjust; so he maintains that it is good to starve and enfeeble the man, and to feast and strengthen the lion and the serpent. But it is better to be governed by a just and divine principle which ought, if possible, to reside in a man's soul."*

Then he tells his pupils an allegory:

> *"Think of a number of persons chained in a cavern. A wall is behind them, and people are passing to and fro the other side of it. The prisoners can't see these people, but the shadow of*

things they carry on their heads is cast on the wall in front of the prisoners. Now, suppose that one of the prisoners were loosed and taken up to the daylight; he would gradually get used to real things, not shadows. There would then be just the same difference between him and the prisoners in the cavern that there is between educated and half-educated people. The purpose of education is to turn round the soul in order that the eye of the soul, or reason, may be directed to real things not shadows. In education we are seeking the form of Good, how to act wisely."

Plato complains that professors of education pretend to infuse into the mind a knowledge of which it was destitute, just as if they were attempting to instil sight into blinded eyes. In reality, he says, there is a faculty residing in the soul of each person – an instrument enabling each of us to learn. The aim of education is to make people, having this faculty, to look in the right direction. The pleasures of eating etc. are earth-born weights, which keep the soul turned on things below, and enslave the soul to the three-headed monster, the body. If from earliest childhood people were released from these snares, and turned round to look at true objects, then men would have as keen an eye for the pursuit of such objects as they now have for earthly and bodily ones. Then people will be really rich – not in gold but in a wise and virtuous life, the wealth essential to a happy man.

A few of the studies Plato suggests are, not reading, but gymnastics, music, astronomy. The two balance each other – the one strengthens the character, and the other makes it gentle and orderly. They make a person brave and temperate. He would especially teach arithmetic and geometry, because they lead us towards truth. His pupil is evidently afraid he is advocating useless studies; but Plato laughs and says:

"It is of more real importance that in these studies an organ of our souls is being purged from the blindness and quickened from the deadness occasioned by other pursuits – an organ whose preservation is of more importance than a thousand eyes, because only by it can truth and the real nature of good be seen."

As a coping-stone to these studies, he would have dialectics. These are the things he would teach. Now, as how to teach.

Care must be taken to convey instruction in such a shape as not to make it compulsory on the child to learn because no study remains rooted in the memory which has been acquired by the mind under compulsion. Hence, you must train children to their studies in a playful manner, without any air of constraint, and with the further object of discerning more readily the natural bent of their respective characters. From his experience of Athenian boys he says the immortality of the soul appeared to him to receive decisive proof from the rapidity from which boys learnt. For they seized on knowledge so readily that they seemed to have come from a previous life, and to be picking up again on what they knew before, and not learning something new.

No head work can be done whilst the children are learning riding and the art of war and doing violent exercise. They must be released from these before their studies begin, for weariness and sleep are enemies to study. Alas, for our children! If one of these Athenians walked through our streets, we would think a god had descended among us. What of our half-timers?

Bodily exercises are an important test of character. At about twenty all the detached studies must be brought within the compass of a single survey, to show the co-relation which exists between them and the nature of real existence. The real dialectician divests himself of his eyes and his other senses and advances in company with truth towards real existence.

Plato insists on one thing – that is, that a child is never too young to begin its education; that this even begins before it is born, in the suitable marriage of its parents. Can you not feel that Plato is not dead, but yet speaks to us? All through the 2,000 years since he lived, people have from time to time been his disciples, and have passed on his message to our day, so that Pestalozzi, influenced by Rousseau, was through him influenced by Plato.

PESTALOZZI

John Pestalozzi was born in 1746, and came to manhood at the time of the French Revolution. He was brought up with love and tender care by his widowed mother and a faithful old servant, and he used to stay in a country village with his grandfather, a good minister. His friends at college shared his enthusiasm for plain living and high thinking, and from reading Rousseau he came to think so much of a simple life that he gave up the law and took to farming. He married Anna Schultheiss, who was as good and devoted as himself. They were shocked at the degraded state of the peasantry round their farm, and he asked himself what the children needed to raise them.

"The thing was not that they should know what they did not know, but that they should behave as they did not behave."

They must be taught not only to respect their elders, but themselves, and if they could be made conscious that they were loved and cared for their hearts would open, and give back love and respect in return.

So he resolved to take into his house some of the very poorest children. Think of the trial to him and his wife, with their little boy, to have twenty of those in the house. He treated them as his own children. They worked with him in gardens and fields, and in winter in the house. Very little time was given to separate lessons. He held that talking should come before reading and writing, and practised them in conversations on subjects taken from their everyday life. They also repeated passages from the Bible till they knew them by heart. In a few months the appearance of these poor little children had entirely changed. Though fed only on bread and vegetables, they looked strong and hearty, and their faces gained an expression of cheerfulness, frankness and intelligence which till then had been totally wanting. They made good progress with their manual work, as well as with the associated lessons, and took pleasure in both. In all they said and did they seemed to show their consciousness of their benefactor's kind care of them.

The first attempt at teaching is the key to Pestalozzi's life-task. He was equally great as a thinker and a doer. However, he was a bad manager, and his farm got into the hands of creditors; he continued to live there, but in extreme poverty. In 1800 he wrote to his friend Zschokke:

*"For thirty years my life has been a well-nigh hopeless
struggle against the most frightful poverty . . .for thirty years
I have had to forego many of the barest necessaries of life, and
have had to shun the society of my fellow-men from sheer lack
of decent clothes. Many and many a time have I gone without
a dinner, or eaten in bitterness a dry crust of bread on the road,
at a time when even the poorest were seated round a table."*
He could well say: " *I desired nothing else then and I desire
nothing else now but the welfare of the people whom I love
and whom I feel to be miserable, as few feel them to be
miserable, because I have with them borne their sufferings as
few have borne them."*

He wrote several books which brought him fame and honour, but not
money. His greatest work was *'Leonard and Gertrude'*, a delightful story
in which one finds his thoughts and education clearly stated.

In his second school at Stanz – he was then fifty – he gathered together
about eighty boys and girls of all ages, left orphans by the war, all incredibly
neglected and degraded, and in six months trained and changed them as
eighteen years earlier he had trained and changed the little peasant children
round Neuhof.

In what did his power exist? This model teacher had everything against
him – thick, indistinct speech, bad writing, ignorance of drawing, scorn of
grammatical learning. He had studied various branches of natural history,
but without any particular attention either to classification or terminology.
He could not do a long sum, for years had read no books, but instead of
knowledge, which any young man can acquire in a year or two, he
understood thoroughly what most masters are ignorant of – the mind of man
and the laws of its development, human affections and the art of rousing
and ennobling them. He maintained that love was only useful in the
education of men when in conjunction with fear: for they must learn to root
out thorns and thistles, which they never do of their own accord, but only
under compulsion and in consequence of training. Pestalozzi wrote:

"I have proved that it is not regular work that stops the development of so many poor children, but the turmoil and irregularity of their lives, the privations they endure, the excesses they indulge in when opportunity offers, the wild rebellious passions so seldom restrained, and the hopelessness to which they are so often a prey. I have proved that children after having lost health, strength and courage in a life of idleness and mendicity have, when once set to regular work, quickly recovered their health and spirits and grown rapidly. I have found that when taken out of their abject condition they soon become kindly, trustful and sympathetic, that even the most degraded of them are touched by kindness and that the eyes of the child who has been steeped in misery grow bright with pleasure and surprise when, after years of hardship, he sees a gentle friendly hand stretched out to help him. I am convinced that when a child's heart has been touched the consequences will be great for his development and entire moral character."

One who had been his pupil wrote:

"We loved him, we all loved him for he loved us all. We loved him so warmly that when some time passed without our seeing him we were quite troubled about it and when he again appeared we could not take our eyes off him."

As a comment on this we may say with Channing that:

" . . . on the contrary, a child compelled for six hours each day to see the countenance and hear the voice of an unfeeling, petulant, passionate, unjust teacher is placed in a school of vice."

The Government examiner of one of his schools wrote a public letter to Pestalozzi:

" The surprising progress of your little scholars of various capacities shows plainly that everyone is good for something, if the teacher knows how to get at his abilities, and develop them according to the laws of psychology. By your method of teaching you have proved how to lay the groundwork of instruction in such a way that it may afterwards support what is built on it . . . Between the ages of five and eight – a period in which, according to the system of torture enforced hitherto, children have learnt to know their letters, to spell and read – your children have not only accomplished all this with a success as yet unknown, but the best of them have already distinguished themselves by their good writing, drawing, and calculating. In them all you have been able to arouse and excite a liking for history, natural history, mensuration, geography, etc. that future teachers must find their task a far easier one if they only know how to make good use of the preparatory stage the children have gone through with you."

Pestalozzi says:

"If we desire to aid the poor man – the very lowest among the people – it can be done in one way only. That is by changing his schools into true places of education, in which the moral, physical, and intellectual powers which God has put into our nature may be drawn out, so that the man may be enabled to live a life such as a man should live. Thus, and thus only, does the man – whom in God's wide world nobody helps and nobody can help – learn to help himself."

This is the end of my story, and the moral is, how can we educate?

CONCLUSION

My purpose in this last part of my lecture is to show that education in the home and at school are the same in aim, and if either mother or teacher forget this, the child will stand a poor chance. The mother must not think she has nothing to do with books, and the teacher must not concern herself only with book learning. Both must wish that the child's mind (or soul, or reason) should grow in strength and discernment, so that it can never be enslaved to the three-headed monster – the body. The mother must never forget that books are a help to this, if through them we can penetrate to the mind of the author, and live over again, with the great of all ages, true and beautiful thoughts, great deeds, or the fun and magic of the old fairy tales. The teacher must never forget that books are only a help. She (or he) must bring into the school-room a large and sympathetic mind for all the realities of life generally, and for the particular circumstances of the life of the locality. She cannot do better than get the spirit of a well-ordered family into her school, putting herself in the place of the wise, patient, loving mother.

The task of education is necessarily begun by the mother. There are few helps to a child to develop well in the terribly bad surroundings of the big towns, but a good mother may save her children anywhere. Having their love, the mother will find it easy to make them obedient, and she should set to work to form good habits in them. The Duke of Wellington said: *"Habit a second nature? Habit is ten times nature."* and he was thinking of how a soldier is made by drill and discipline. Bacon says: *"Education is but an early custom."* This, however, is only half the truth. Good habits are an important part of education, but we must not lose sight of the central fact that the young human being is a new creation, with possibilities of development of which we know nothing, and in matters of fashion and non-essentials it should choose its own habits. Everyone should follow his own opinions and tastes in small matters. Mothers, do not try to make your children just like everyone else. Some good habits by which the child's will can be strengthened are making it do the same think every day – not giving it a 'piece' at odd times, but making it wait for meals, when the whole family sit down together with washed hands, and not moving till the meal is finished. A child should go to bed and get up at a fixed hour every day. A child should never be allowed to overhear what its parents do not wish repeated and then be ordered 'not to tell' – it should never learn 'not to tell' – and, of course, if the parents have intelligent interests and pure unselfish aims the child will be helped to that virtue which is knowledge. You may smile at my telling you things which you know better than I, but I do it to make you understand that teaching at school must be on the same plan, and should, as I have said, have for its aim the strengthening and development of the child's mind – and minds (or characters) may be as varied as the flowers in a garden, and all equally right – and fitting it to live and work as a harmonious and helpful part of the great social order, the commonwealth.

The strictness of the devoted, self-sacrificing mother should be the pattern for the teacher. An atmosphere of love must surround the growing being; it is as necessary to it as sunshine and water to a plant. It will seldom be necessary to correct a child who feels he is loved, and I think the teacher may give each child in a large class the feeling that it is loved, by a bright, sympathetic manner and a word now and then to one or another of the children, if possible to the plainest and least attractive, whom the teacher will love most, because she cannot *like* it; it has lost so much of the aristocracy of childhood, and she pities it. Even wickedness and stubbornness she may regard as disease – deformity of the mind – for which strong remedies are needed, but for which the child is to be much more pitied than blamed. I would venture to suggest that once or twice during the week she should have a children's hour for her class, when the children should be encouraged to express their thoughts. She will find that a good many of them have burdens to bear which are too heavy for childish shoulders, that physically and mentally the parents' influence is all wrong. But even then she need not despair of educating the child. I think that childlike and right impulses survive a good deal of misleading, and that when the child's mind comes in contact with the teacher's, those impulses will be aroused, and the child may be all the stronger and more intelligent for having *chosen* that it will be right. The right atmosphere of a school-room implies that the teacher and the children understand each other, and this will give life and interest to the dullest routine work. I think the teacher should interest the children in herself, just enough to make them feel they too may grow strong and clever and enlightened. She must never let a child feel despondent and diffident, or think that it has got to get just enough education for a working-man's child, and no more. There is no class in education; there is only true and false education, the same for all. In America all classes send their children to the same elementary schools, the millionaire's and the navvy's child sit side by side, and this is right, and should be a safeguard against the error (the crime I might almost say) of some teachers, of looking down on the children, as if they were inferior.

The talks I have suggested between teachers and pupils would develop into lessons on morals. This teaching must be convincing or it will do harm. Appeal more to the child's reason than to its emotions. Thoughts grow stronger, emotions weaker with use. Subjects for talk might be; altruism and citizenship, showing how anti-social every sort of sin and selfishness is; honesty, honour, thrift, habit, industry; temperance and self-restraint, showing that the body is the worst of masters; care and reverence for the body, to make it as beautiful and healthy as possible; the uses of money, which should include an explanation of how money came to be a medium of exchange, and how it represents so much labour which others are willing to do for us, in exchange for labour we do for them, and the consequent dishonesty of asking credit. Strenuous efforts should be made to reach children in the elementary schools to govern themselves. Do not *make* them obey. Teach them to be orderly and obedient, because they have reflected that school could not go on if they were not; and respectful, because they *feel* respect for the thoroughness and devotion of the teacher. These lessons must not be given out of a handbook. The teacher must have thought them out and convinced *herself* first and, if the size of the class did not make it impossible, the children should be encouraged to ask questions. In the same way, object-lessons should be made experimental and convincing – an exercise of thought not of memory.

One thing the teacher must know and make her pupils feel – the unity of life. However many subjects she teaches, she must make them know there is only one subject – mind, life, the life of the universe – and that separation from this one life, through pride, selfishness, competition, is death. Froebel sought to teach this through symbolism: his first gift, the ring, is a type of life – no beginning and no end – and all parts of it equal and necessary. By the time they leave the kindergarten, the knowledge of this unity should have become a habit of mind with the children; they should have become social beings. A savage is a person who has not learnt this, and a savage in a crowded room is ten times more savage and terrible than one in the woods. I am afraid there are amongst us some such savages who lead genteel, orderly lives.

As to lessons and the examiner, you have to find employment for four or five hours every day; and the children, full of goodwill, thought and observation, will easily learn what is necessary without finding books a bugbear. In the higher standards earnest efforts should be made to give pupils a right estimate of and love of books, so that when they leave school at fourteen they may ask for more – like Oliver Twist – and take advantage of the technical and other evening continuation schools. If education were like this, working people would not feel that their children had no more use for it than a cow has for clogs, and grudge the time spent in getting through their standards. There would be so much besides standards and if they saw the children growing daily more gracious and strong and clever, they would know that they were getting a good return for their sacrifice in keeping them at school.

Have I said enough to suggest to you that there is pressing need for us to turn over a new leaf, in our thoughts first, and in our actions afterwards? This new-old education is a sacred thing. Human nature has always the same needs and possibilities; only from time to time people lose sight of what might be. So many people in the Potteries are undersized and sickly that we almost forget how big and beautiful and strong people might be, and it is so with the mind. We bundle the children off to school, and go about our work and our pleasure without giving them another thought. A good many of them grow up foolish, idle and dissipated, and we wonder why it is, when they have been kept so many years at school and had so much spent on them. Dr. Thring, headmaster of a great public school for gentlemen's sons, said there was no teaching, and there could be no teaching any more – law and public opinion made it impossible. We do not want to lay down the law for teachers; it is a skilled trade and we have much respect and sympathy with those who follow it in an earnest, self-sacrificing spirit. But let us concern ourselves with law and public opinion and try to know what we aim at, and I do not doubt we shall get it.

Young Workers in a Potbank.

4. First Blood

Essex Street, London EC2
20th March 1907

Early in the morning of 20th March 1907 Sarah Benett reported to the Essex Hall in Essex Street, off The Strand, for her first Meeting as a member of the 'Women's Social and Political Union'.

Essex Street had for long been associated with religious dissention and social reform. The Unitarian Movement in Britain had first established itself there and the Essex Hall, built in 1886 on the site of the original Unitarian Chapel, became their headquarters. They also let the Hall out as a meeting place for several, mainly radical, organisations including the 'Fabian Society'.

On this day it had been reserved for a meeting of the WSPU and a large crowd of women from all over the country had assembled. They were told that, later in the day, they would all move to the Caxton Hall in Westminster where a further meeting was to be held prior to the planned action. In the meantime, they were to be instructed by Mrs. Pethick-Lawrence and Miss Annie Kenney in the basic aims of the Movement and in the tactics for causing the maximum amount of nuisance to the authorities. An ample spread of food was provided for those attending the meeting.

**Essex Hall c.1918.
The Hall, together with much of Essex Street, was destroyed by a V1 'Doodlebug' in 1944 and has now been rebuilt on the same site.**

Caxton Hall, c.1890. Built originally as the Westminster Town Hall, Caxton Hall played a central role in the movement for women's suffrage.

WESTMINSTER CITY COUNCIL

After this induction, the women were told to proceed to Caxton Hall. As Sarah was familiar with the streets of London, she was put in charge of three women from Preston in Lancashire whom she found to be a troublesome charge as their attendance at the meeting appeared to have been inspired more by the prospect of a jolly day out in London rather than a commitment to the cause.

> *"I took them with me to Caxton Hall. I think we took a bus from Charing Cross. I don't know what their ideas were, they did not appear to feel the solemnity of the occasion and, before getting there, they insisted on buying picture post cards or sending telegrams, which betrayed our errand and we got much stared at."* [2]

At Caxton Hall there was another handsome spread of food for the delegates and the meeting started at 3 pm with Mrs. Pankhurst in the Chair.

Impassioned speeches were made by her and her daughter Christabel, Mrs. Despard, Mrs. Pethick-Lawrence and Miss Annie Kenney who was dressed in her mill clogs and shawl to emphasise the classless constitution of the Union. The purpose of the Meeting, they were told, was to adopt a resolution to be taken and handed personally to the Prime Minister:

> *"The meeting expresses its indignation at the refusal of the Prime Minister to grant time for the adjourned discussion of Mr. Dickinson's Women's Enfranchisement Bill, and calls upon Sir Henry Campbell-Bannerman to give effect to his own declared convictions on this question by the immediate introduction of a Government measure to remove the disability of sex."*

As speech followed speech, each more militant and stirring than the one before, the mood of the meeting became increasingly inflamed and a torrent of cheers and hand clapping greeted the proposal.

"Rise up! Rise up women!" Mrs. Pankhurst exhorted them from the platform and was answered by a roar of voices: *"We will, we will, NOW!"*

"And who will undertake the duty of taking this resolution to the Prime Minister in the House of Commons?"

"I will," shouted Lady Harberton from the crowd, *"I will take it to the Prime Minister if this meeting so desires and shall consider it an honour to do so."*

Florence Pomeroy, Viscountess Harberton, a supporter of Women's Rights though better known for her involvement in the campaign for Rational Dress and the rights of women cyclists.

LADYHARBERTON.COM

"*Lady Harberton will lead the way to Westminster,*" shouted Mrs. Pankhurst, "*to the street and form yourselves behind her.*"

Lady Harberton with three women from Manchester was to lead the march with Sarah and her three women from Preston right behind her. However, Sarah's charges seemed more interested in remaining at the buffet than forming up outside and she had to talk to them severely, reminding them of the reason they were there.

> "*The three women seemed to have forgotten everything they had been told and not to intend to leave the Hall. However I got them together soon enough to follow Lady Harburton* (sic) *closely.*" [2]

Before leaving the Hall on her first operation, Sarah was overcome with the importance of the crusade on which she was about to embark:

> "*. . . before getting out of the Hall, I experienced a sort of paroxysm of excitement and rage; I think my heart stopped and a mist came before my eyes.*" [2]

The police, who had been observing the Meeting, knew exactly what to expect and were well prepared. As the women surged out of the Hall they were met by a solid block of policemen who forced their way in amongst them, breaking them up into small groups and preventing any chance of an orderly procession.

Lady Harberton, waving the Petition above her head, rallied her supporters to surround her as she shouted her defiance to the police cordon and reaffirmed her determination to proceed with it to the House of Commons. Eventually the officer-in-charge agreed that she, alone, should be allowed through but her supporters must remain where they were.

This met with an attempt by the crowd to break through to Victoria Street but the police anticipated the move and the surge of bodies was blocked by an unbroken line of policemen. The '*London Daily News*' described what followed:

"Then the struggle commenced. They banded themselves together in little groups of five or six and all constitutional methods failed to separate them. They pulled and struggled, hustled and pushed and for some five minutes the police had a bad time. 'Break them up, Boys! Break them up!' yelled the Inspector above the din. In a body the police bore down on the groups of women but met a stubborn resistance. Across the road and back again surged the struggling mass. Down the street cabs and carriages and tooting motor cars became entangled in the melee." [15]

Eventually the women were allowed to filter through to Victoria Street and, waving banners and shouting slogans, commenced their march towards the Houses of Parliament where they were stopped again by a police blockade. The stalemate was temporarily broken when a rousing cheer greeted the dramatic arrival of Annie Kenney in a hansom cab, standing posed like Boadicea in her mill shawl and clogs, one hand defiantly reaching for the sky as she urged the crowd to *'Rise up!'*.

Later, a horse-drawn omnibus full of seemingly innocent spectators was allowed through the crowd so the passengers could get a better view of the proceedings. However, the 'spectators' turned out to be a large party of Lancashire mill girls down from the North to support the suffragettes. At a given signal, they left the omnibus and made a rush at the police cordon.

Meanwhile, Lady Harberton had arrived at the Strangers' Door of the House of Commons and asked to see Sir Charles McLaren. She was told that he was not in the House so she said she would see Mr. Keir Hardie or Mr. Philip Snowden instead.

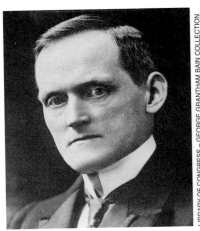

Philip Snowden MP (1864-1937), later first Viscount Snowden and the first Labour Chancellor of the Exchequer.

National Union of Women's Suffrage Societies

GREAT MEETING

. IN .

QUEEN'S HALL

LANGHAM PLACE, W.,

On Tuesday, 26th March, 1907.

At 8 p.m. (Doors Open at 7)
IN SUPPORT OF

WOMEN'S SUFFRAGE

On the eve of the Resolution to be moved by SIR CHARLES McLAREN, Bart, M.P., in the House of Commons.

CHAIRMAN:

MRS. HENRY FAWCETT, LL.D.,

(President N.U.W.S.S.)

SPEAKERS:

THE LADY FRANCES BALFOUR,
LADY BAMFORD SLACK,
MISS FRANCES STERLING,

(Joint Hon Sec. N.U.W.S.S.)

MR. CAMERON CORBETT, M.P.,
MR. G. BERNARD SHAW,
MR. PHILIP SNOWDEN, M.P.,

AND OTHERS.

Area Stalls (Reserved and Numbered), **5s.**, **3s.**, and **2s.** Grand Circle (Reserved and Numbered): Front Row, **5s.**; Other Rows, **3s.** and **2s.** Reserved till 8 p.m., but not Numbered: Area, **1s.**; Balcony, **6d.**

NOTE.—**12** Tickets for the price of **10** to any part of the Hall.

All applications for Tickets to be made to the Secretary,
25, VICTORIA STREET, WESTMINSTER, S.W.

Philip Snowden was known to be sympathetic to their cause and was due to speak on the following Tuesday at a meeting to be held at the Queen's Hall in support of women's suffrage. He came to the door and explained that she had no chance of seeing the Prime Minister to present the Resolution and, having examined it himself, declared that it did not contain details of the meeting at which the Resolution had been passed so would be considered null and void and would consequently never reach the PM anyway.

Although the principal object of their march had therefore failed, the demonstration outside the House of Commons continued unabated. Among the committed supporters of the cause was one, Patricia Woodlock from Liverpool, who had only recently been released from prison for a previous disturbance.

"Hatless and energetic, she slipped half through a gap in the police lines opposite St. Margaret's as a police inspector

stepped aside to give some instructions. A constable was too quick for her, and when she tried to push through forcibly she was taken by the waist and thrust back." [15]

The report, in the '*London Daily News*', of her continued efforts could just as well have been a description of a pack of rugby forwards battling desperately to get the ball over a heavily-defended goal line:

Mabel Capper (left) and Patricia Woodlock (right) at a Meeting in Manchester in 1908

MUSEUM OF LONDON

90

"Then ensued a series of heavy charges, for Miss Woodlock is a well built young woman, with strength in her limbs. She went from end to end of the line in an effort to find an opening, and was so persistent that at last the inspector ordered her arrest." [15]

As Sarah emerged from the Caxton Hall with her three Preston followers, she had had her first experience of militant action:

"We had hardly got outside when a body of the heaviest policemen fell on us and scattered us in all directions, by shouldering their way in between us. They and the public and the suffragettes became a dense mass and we ceased to be a procession; each one of us was intent on extricating herself. I adopted Annie Kenney's advice and knocked off the helmets of several policemen but, as I was always behind my victim, they did not feel certain which was the culprit and I escaped into Tothill Street. . . . I walked quietly on till I got to the cordon of police guarding the entrance to Palace Yard. I noticed that they allowed men to pass through but, when I attempted to follow, I was stopped. I protested against distinguishing between members of the public and said I was in my right but, of course, it was no use; they whispered to each other: "that's her" and I think I was recognised as their assailant at Caxton Hall. They arrested me and two of them took me to Cannon Row holding both my arms as if I were a most dangerous person." [2]

At Cannon Row Sarah was charged with obstructing the police and was then taken to the billiard room where, together with about 80 other women, she waited to be bailed. Mrs. Pethick-Lawrence arrived for this at about 7 pm and, having given an undertaking to be peaceful, the prisoners were released and returned to Caxton Hall where a fresh Meeting was to be held.

First Blood

Sarah sought out Christabel Pankhurst and told her that she was prepared to engage her own Counsel if she thought it would do any good. However, a barrister, Mr. Campbell, was appointed for her defence without further consultation who spoke to her, very briefly, before her case was heard at Rochester Row the next morning.

> *"Counsel was employed for me without my being consulted but I felt, at this first trial, that it was a mistake – the barrister was not carefully enough instructed to bring out telling points and you cannot speak at all if you were not defending your own case. In no case would a barrister view the case from a suffragette's standpoint and so, not only were facts often distorted, but motives were still more often ignored. This was the first and last time I voluntarily employed Counsel."* [2]

At this time, prison sentences were divided into First, Second or Third Division with the First Division offering the most lenient regime and the highest level of privileges. Sarah received the standard sentence given to suffragettes at that time – two weeks imprisonment in the First Division. After sentencing she was taken to the cells below the court where she spent several hours locked up with *"drunken and disreputable women"* though she and the other suffragettes received visits from friends who brought them food and writing materials which were handed through the bars.

In the speech she made after her release, Sarah later said that it was in that moment that she realised, as never before or since, the awful possibilities of captivity when you were handed over to the custody of chance people and had no voice and no redress. In due course, she and the other suffragettes were collected by a 'Black Maria' and taken to Holloway Prison.

This grim, castle-like Victorian building had been a women-only prison since four years earlier in 1903 when the notorious 'Finchley Baby Farmers', Amelia Sach and Annie Walters, who collected unwanted babies and murdered them, had been hanged by Henry Pierrepoint in the only double execution of women in modern times. The prison was the usual

Holloway Prison.

destination for convicted suffragettes and therefore came to play a symbolic role in the struggle for women's rights. Despite their constant demands to be treated as political prisoners, suffragettes were regarded as run-of-the-mill common criminals though they did, at this time, enjoy the relatively easier conditions of the First Division.

Of her first experience of imprisonment Sarah wrote:

"I suffered horribly during that fortnight; after a nerve-wracking day in Court there is nothing imaginary in the punishment of being put in a narrow cell inside Black Maria and jolted away to Holloway; and on arrival there, being locked in a reception cell and, after being kept there for what seemed ages, being ordered out and kept standing about for all sorts of formalities to be gone through for fresh ages; and finally, having to precede, laden with a pair of sheets and a towel, (you never follow because every instant you are not under lock and key in your cell you are in custody), an

UNDAUNTED !

Oh Justice what crimes are practised in thy name,
To the Law's discredit and the Nation's shame !

A Suffragette in Prison.
Poster published as a supplement to *"The Suffragist"* October 1909.

impassive, or perhaps a rude and irritable, wardress till you reach your cell; it may be on the second or third floor. As soon as you are inside the key is turned in the lock and the helpless baffled feeling returns with ten-fold force.

"The horror of imprisonment at once overwhelmed some of our women and their friends had to pay their fines. A great many others, especially the rougher working women, languished after two or three days; the solitude overwhelmed them and they simply collapsed finding no resource in books, everything showing how uneven punishment in a cast-iron system is.

"In those days we used to be drilled like soldiers to do everything with minute exactness – our plank bedsteads had to be stood up against the wall during the day and the bedding rolled up together, exactly according to order. We were given sandstone and a flannel rag to keep our tins bright; all this had to be done to the satisfaction of the wardress before 10 o'clock when we were taken into the yard to walk round and round, about 30 ft apart and never speaking for an hour, returning to our cells at 11 and being kept in them till 10 next morning.

"During the afternoon we were on view. No windows opened in those days; they were grimy on the outside and a little tired air came in through ventilators in the wall. I asked if they were ever cleaned and was told that during fire drill the hose played on them. We had a deal stool, with no back to it, to sit on and one could find little or no relief to cruel back ache by sitting or lying on the cement floor; and if you were caught doing this you were scolded. There is another form of torture in prison life which continues still though we have reformed as much. You may smuggle a watch into your cell and it is a great joy to you. Without one you never know what time it is, but with one you quickly find out that the prison is not run for you, but for the 'personnel' of the prison, who apparently are all quite

independent of each other. The Governor, the Chaplain the Doctor, the Matron, the Head Wardress, the Visiting Magistrates all need you though you have no use for half of them. All have to see the prisoners; you are the reason for their pay and position and they flounce into the cells, without any warning, till it seemed to you that you were 'on view' every afternoon, not for any benefit you might derive from it but because you had to come into their reports.

"The Governor, Matron and Doctor are bound to see you every day when you are refusing your food. We were then an interesting novelty the Chaplain came to each of us with his notebook and asked: "are you educated?" One answer was: "I was a student of Girton. You know what a university education is and may call it education; I don't." I answered: "I think I may say 'yes' as I am a good German and French scholar and widely read and generally cultured." The Chaplain was quite chatty after that; he reminded me that in his book 'International Law' Sir H. Mayne brought out that if any reform was granted without people ardently desiring it, and fighting for it, it might remain a dead letter and that therefore all our work and sufferings were a gain, and were paving the way for an intelligent use of the vote when it did come. I got the character of being of a happy disposition.

"The uncertainty of it all is almost torture. You may be left alone for hours when you particularly wanted to speak to someone, or you might be perpetually interrupted when you felt you needed rest and quiet though now a wardress is not sent in advance to say: "Stand up for the Governor", they have had to drop many such customs as they have become unworkable through us." [2]

By 10 o'clock on the evening of the 20th the fire of the demonstration had been quenched and a succession of tired women began boarding omnibuses to return home. A few were still determined to continue their protest and

A contemporary postcard showing three of the most renowned suffragette leaders, all of whom served prison sentences – *(from left)* **Emmeline Pankhurst, Annie Kenney and Emmeline Pethick Lawrence in the 'Suffragette Taxi' driven by Bill Ropley, the Pethick-Lawrence's gardener.**

one group, watched by Mr. Gladstone and Mr. Lloyd George among other MPs, attempted to storm Downing Street. Their progress was blocked by the police who, to the suffragettes' dismay, had avoided making arrests wherever possible. They already had over 70 women in custody and were perhaps reluctant to overload the system further but the main reason for their forbearance was the knowledge that, to a suffragette, an arrest was a badge of honour. Mounted police were deployed to disperse the final remnants of the demonstrators and by 10.30 pm peace prevailed again in Westminster.

Demonstrators arrested in Westminster on 20th March 1907 with the towns from which they came.

Birmingham
Mrs. Lacon
Mrs. Smith

Bolton
Mrs. Ford

Bournemouth
Miss Wright, R.

Bradford
Mrs. Barrett
Miss King Townsend
Miss Varley

Burslem
Miss Benett, Sarah

Chelmsford
Miss Aves

Croydon
Mrs. Holmes

Dewsbury
Mrs. Cooper

Edinburgh
Miss Graves

Glamorgan
Mrs. Jenkins

Glasgow
Mrs. Montgomery
Miss Smith, Frances
Miss Smith, Jessie

Halifax
Mrs. Connelly
Mrs. Draper

Miss Saltonstall
Mrs. Willson

Hebden Bridge
Miss Berkeley, Lizzie
Miss Cobbe, Lilian

Hitchin
Mrs. Impey

Huddersfield
Miss Brooks
Mrs. Hollawell
Miss Hopson
Mrs. Pinnace
Mrs. Pogson
Miss Scawthorne
Miss Thewley, Dora

Liverpool
Mrs. Morrissey
Mrs. Roberts
Miss Woodlock

London
Mrs. Arncliffe-Sennett
Miss Bigg
Miss Bray, W.
Miss Cimino
Mrs. Clayton
Miss Clifford, Cecilia
Miss Clyde
Mrs. Crumming
Dr. Hardie, Mabel
Miss Ibbotson
Miss Jerome, Veronica
Miss Kirwen
Miss Lamb, A.
Miss Leigh
Miss Lillingstone
Mrs. Mitchell, Eileen

Mrs. Morrow
Madame Naici-Peters
Miss New
Miss Rozier, Emma
Mr. Orage, A.R.
Miss Sedley
Mrs. Smith, Peter
Miss Toyne
Mrs. Townsend
Mrs. Winton Evans

Manchester
Mrs. Chatterton
Miss Marsden
Miss Milne
Mrs. Mitchell
Mrs. Rawle

Merthyr Tydfil
Miss Arxott

Newcastle-on-Tyne
Mrs. Atkinson

Preston
Miss Armstrong
Miss Barrows
Mrs. Jackson

Rochdale
Mrs. Sheard
Miss Sholefield
Miss Wilkinson

Sheffield
Mrs. Higgins
Mrs. Lockwood

Wolverhampton
Mrs. Price
Miss Sproson

5. "The Split"

40-42 Chandos Place, London, Thursday 4th April 1907

The 'Eustace Miles Restaurant' in Chandos Place, at the western end of Covent Garden, had become a popular rendezvous with suffragettes. The link was vegetarianism; many suffragettes had adopted a vegetarian diet and this restaurant was promoted as a 'food reform' establishment with an entirely meat- and fish-free menu. In E.M. Forster's '*Howards End*' it is the restaurant where health conscious Margaret Schlegel introduces conservative Henry Wilcox to 'healthy food'.

Eustace Hamilton Miles, educated at Marlborough and Cambridge, was a noted sportsman who had held the title of 'Amateur Real Tennis Champion of England' for several years. The following year he was to win an Olympic Silver Medal and, throughout a long sporting career, he held several titles in racquets and squash. He was also what today would be called a 'health freak' and he attributed his fitness to a vegetarian diet.

In 1906 together with his wife Hattie and several partners including George Bernard Shaw, E.F. Benson, and the headmaster of Eton, he opened his restaurant in Chandos Place. Formed at around the same time as the Women's Social and Political Union, the two grew up together and the restaurant, with its menu of such dishes as cauliflower cheese, vegetable soup and french bean

Eustace Miles whose vegetarian restaurant in Chandos Place was very popular with suffragettes.

HTTP://WWW.VAM.AC.UK/USERS/NODE/8711

Edith Craig, daughter of actress Ellen Terry and women's rights news vendor.

omelettes, became the favourite eating place for several suffragette leaders including Sylvia Pankhurst.

Living in nearby Bedford Street, Edith Craig, daughter of Ellen Terry the actress and a well-known theatre director and producer in her own right, was also a fervent supporter of women's suffrage and could often be seen selling copies of *'Votes for Women'* outside the door of the restaurant.

Vegetarianism in the early years of the 20th century was becoming very trendy. Another form of bucking and outraging established practices naturally appealed to young women of independent spirit – the same women who enthusiastically embraced the cause for women's rights – and many of them were declared vegetarians before they became suffragists.

Another stimulus was the writings of the respected Irish academic and poet Margaret, or Gretta, Cousins who urged women to rebel against the tyranny of cookery and household chores which, she claimed, deprived them of the time and leisure they needed to address much more important intellectual and social matters. She exhorted women to abandon the cooking of time-consuming meat-, poultry- and fish-based meals and switch to a diet of simple grain, fruit and nuts, advice which undoubtedly endeared her to many men who regarded a proper cooked meal on their return from work as a right.

WOMAN AND HER SPHERE

Margaret (Gretta) Cousins who urged women to switch to a vegetarian diet.

100

So it was that Eustace Miles's restaurant was chosen as the venue for a WSPU breakfast for the prisoners being released after their sentences for the March 20th demonstrations.

Before attending this breakfast meeting, Sarah deposited her bags at the flat of a cousin who had offered to put her up for a night or two after her release from Holloway. She found that everything seemed different after the confinement of the cell in which she had spent the past fortnight:

> *"I remember how very spacious everything seemed when I was liberated; air and colour and space seemed everywhere, the walls of my cousin's very ordinary rooms seemed quite a long way off – I returned there after a breakfast at Eustace Miles's. Medals had not been invented in those days; most of us made little speeches – those to whom speech making was familiar, the best."* [2]

Sarah told the assembled audience of her actions and emotions during what had been her first operation and many expressed surprise and admiration that a lady of such unusually advanced years, she was 56, should have voluntarily suffered the privations of a prison sentence for her beliefs.

> *"A most interesting document was presented to me shortly after – a declaration of approval and admiration from socialist women accompanied by a letter from Ethel Snowden. Mrs. P. Lawrence wrote with this and it is significant that on the official W.S.P.U. paper a great many names appear but not that of Mrs. Pankhurst."* [2]

The campaign and her subsequent prison sentence had taken a lot out of Sarah and she felt the need to return to familiar surroundings and recoup for a time:

> *"I returned to the Potteries to fight against the negation of living, which was then the lot of every single woman, however*

Elizabeth Wolstenholme Elmy.

WIKIMEDIA – PUBLIC DOMAIN

skillfully she might conceal the fact. My life was very full, I was Hon. Sec. of a Boarding Out Committee and I had a number of pauper children to look after. I gave money to support strikes among the Potters and made little speeches at their meetings. I attended Co-operative Guild Meetings and on 17th June I went, as their delegate, to the C.W. Guild Meeting at Darlington." [2]

Though Sarah was again leading a very busy life in the Midlands and had renewed her association with the education authorities, the trades unions and the co-operative movement, the injustice of women's exclusion was still smouldering within her and a visit to Mrs. Wolstenholme Elmy on 4th July 1907 was to rekindle the flames of suffragism.

Elizabeth Clarke Wolstenholme Elmy, who was 74 when Sarah met her, had been denied higher education herself, due to her clergyman father's atavistic views, and had dedicated the rest of her life to opening educational opportunities to women. In addition to founding and running her own boarding school for girls, she was a member of the National Secular Society (NSS), and an ardent feminist and campaigner for women's rights.

> *On 4th July I visited a most charming and clever lady, Mrs. Wolstenholme Elmy, at Congleton, and got again into the wholesome atmosphere of militant suffragism and, on 16th July, I came in contact for the first time with those who were coming to the front in the W.S.P.U.* [2]

Albert Stanley, former coal miner
and Liberal MP for North-West
Staffordshire.

Christabel Pankhurst who stayed
with Sarah in Burslem
for a week in 1907

As Campbell-Bannerman's Liberal government refused to advocate votes for women, it became WSPU policy to oppose, and campaign against, Liberal candidates in elections. One such was Albert Stanley, candidate for North-West Staffordshire, who received opposition from some of the leading WSPU members.

> *I met Christabel Pankhurst at Stoke Station and took her to stay with me at Burslem. I think she was there a week. Meanwhile her sister Adela, Mary Gawthorpe, Annie Kenney, Acta Lamb, Mrs. Drummond and a number of others were staying in the Constituency (N.W. Staffs) to fight the Liberal candidate Albert Stanley. This was an initiation into a new phase of usefulness but the old order was more futile than ever after my taste of militancy. I had been treated seriously enough to be punished. I had reached a higher level than before in being classed, with drunks and disorderlies, as a menace to the State. I had conquered some sort of a place in life, if only*

"The Split"

the place of the criminal! There is a certain dignity in the woman who has lost all sense of decency and self respect; she is revenging herself on society which has wronged or neglected her; her action is self-destruction, but all martyrdom is a form of self-destruction. I had become a rebel, a grand thing! During the autumn I induced two sisters, who kept a china shop, to go to the Town Hall with me and we formally

Three mainstays of the newly-formed Women's Freedom League
from left: **Edith How-Martyn, Charlotte Despard and Emma Sproson.**

> *demanded of the revising barrister to be put on the*
> *parliamentary voters' list. I also stood for the Town Council*
> *but a great many people took a great deal of trouble to keep*
> *me out and my professed supporters, the trades unionists, were*
> *only half hearted; in fact I feel sure the man who acted as my*
> *agent had been got at; he neither worked himself nor got*
> *anyone else to work though heaps of good men were on strike,*
> *and I failed. I was living in a hideous squalid district and I*
> *had nothing to do, but relieve distress.* [2]

So, late in 1907 Sarah left her house and belongings in Burslem with a caretaker and moved back to London where she took lodgings. She attended a meeting of the WSPU at Clements Inn where she learnt that there had been a split in the Union and several prominent members had left to found a new group of their own which they had called the Women's Freedom League (WFL). Having been in the Midlands at the time, Sarah was unaware of the reasons for the split but decided to attend a meeting of the WFL at their headquarters at 18 Buckingham Street so she could judge the issues for herself.

> *"Something jarred on me at Clements Inn and I decided to*
> *throw in my lot with the other party. I had been a member of*
> *the one Society before the 'split' and not being on the spot I*
> *had never discovered why there was a split; now of course I*
> *quickly did."* [2]

There was a number of reasons for the split but the most fundamental of these was the decision of Emmeline Pankhurst and her daughter Christabel to effectively suspend the WSPU constitution. The annual conference was cancelled and it was announced that future decisions would be made by a committee which was to be appointed by the Pankhursts themselves. This move towards autocratic rule was not well received by many members who were, in the main, independent-minded women of spirit who were accustomed to making their own decisions or at least having a say in the way in which their voluntary efforts were to be deployed.

LIBRARY OF CONGRESS – GEORGE GRANTHAM BAIN COLLECTION

WIKIMEDIA – PUBLIC DOMAIN

Charlotte Despard.

Margaret Nevinson.

Secondly, the Independent Labour Party with which the WSPU had previously been allied, had made public its support for universal suffrage which the WSPU did not want; they were simply pressing for women to be subject to the same terms as men with regard to their entitlement to vote and had no argument with the property qualifications then in force which restricted the vote to men of some substance and excluded the vast majority of ordinary working class people. These were seen by many defecting members as a class barrier with which they did not wish to be associated.

Another divergence of opinion was in the attitude of the two organisations towards the use of violence. While the WSPU were prepared to use any means to gain the attention of the public and to achieve their ends, the WFL policy, initially, disallowed the use of violence in favour of mass demonstrations and individual acts of defiance such as members chaining themselves to railings and refusing to co-operate with the authorities in such matters as the national census.

WIKIMEDIA – PUBLIC DOMAIN

FLICKR API – LSE WOMEN'S LIBRARY COLLECTION

Anne Cobden Sanderson.

Helena Normanton (c. 1930)

The acknowledged leader of the women who founded the WFL was Mrs. Charlotte Despard. Six years older than Sarah, she was the daughter of an Ascendancy-Irish Royal Naval commander and sister of John French, later Field Marshal Lord French, first Earl of Ypres who had been Commander-in-Chief of the British Expeditionary Force in 1914 and subsequently Chief of the Imperial General Staff. As a pacifist, supporter of Sinn Fein and a devout Roman Catholic, Charlotte was at odds with her more famous brother at almost every level.

Her definition of democracy differed from that of Emmeline Pankhurst. Despard believed it to be government by the people through elected representatives while Pankhurst believed democracy to be the state which could only come about when total equality had been achieved which could only be reached through inspired and unconstricted leadership – her own.

Other founders of the WFL included Teresa Billington-Greig who had been one of the WSPUs principal speakers and the first suffragette to be

A plaque commemorating 'Red Emma' in her native city of Wolverhampton.

imprisoned in 1906; Edith How-Martyn who had held the office of Joint Secretary of the WSPU and was immediately appointed Honorary Secretary of the WFL; Margaret Nevinson, an academic who was married to a radical journalist with whom she had campaigned for women's suffrage for many years; Anne Cobden-Sanderson a suffragette who had been arrested in 1906 but freed after a protest by George Bernard Shaw; Helena Normanton a teacher who would later become an eminent KC and Emma Sproson, known as 'Red Emma' a Sunday school teacher and member of the ILP. Sproson had become a women's rights activist after she had asked Lord Curzon a question at a public meeting which he had refused to answer because she was a woman. About 70 other women made the switch from WSPU to WFL and the public's proclivity for the new organisation's charter soon became evident with very rapid growth until it had 60 branches throughout the country and a membership of around 4,000 – roughly twice the size of the WSPU.

Although Sarah had often proclaimed her belief in the need for violent protest, the other arguments in favour of the WFL seem to have been sufficiently substantive for her to transfer her allegiance. Her first project as a WFL member was to challenge the legitimacy of man-made laws being enforced upon women in courts officered by men:

> *"I and another went to Clerkenwell Police Court and we quietly took our places amongst the public and listened till a small, terrified woman was placed in the dock. Then I rose and, standing very upright, in a clear loud voice, I protested against the trial of a woman by man-made-laws in a court exclusively officered by men. There was absolute silence and*

everyone listened to me. When I had finished Mr. d'Eyoncourt said: "Remove that woman" but there was no need to remove me; we gathered our things and left the court voluntarily." [2]

Shortly after this, it was decided by the management of the WFL that members, particularly those with a proven ability in debate, should be sent to interview a number of ministers to seek a pledge from each that they would use their vote and influence in support of a Women's Suffrage Bill. It was usual for two WFL members to be sent together and in Sarah's case she was accompanied by a "Miss S.S." to No. 2 Cambridge Square, the home of Captain John Sinclair, Secretary for Scotland.

Sinclair, who was to become the first Baron Pentland the following year, was educated at Wellington and Sandhurst and had served in the Sudan with the 5th Royal Irish Lancers before entering politics. In 1904 he had married Lady Marjorie Gordon, daughter of the 1st Marquess of Aberdeen and Temair, and he was later to become a distinguished Governor of Madras.

Sarah rose early on the morning of 30th January 1908 and was at No. 2 Cambridge Square at 9 am. She knocked on the door which was answered by a maid and asked if Captain Sinclair would see her:

"He assented and we were shown into the dining room the breakfast things were still on the table and Capt. S. quickly joined us. He said no one could give such a pledge but he would write to the W.F.L. We had rather a heated discussion as my instructions were to regard

Captain John Sinclair later first Baron Pentland.

109

*anything but 'yes' as 'no'. I loitered on the doorstep after I
had been shown out wondering how I could possibly begin
holding a meeting in that quiet square. Captain S. came out
and passed us quickly evidently thinking I wanted to speak to
him again. This made things easier as I knew there were no
men in the house; Miss S.S. was there for audience and the
newspaper reporter, who had also been summoned by the
W.F.L., proved to be from the Potteries and knew me well. I
said to him: "please fetch a policeman soon" and, standing
on the doorstep, I began to speak and spoke to an increasing
crowd which at last blocked the Square for nearly two hours.
Several times the policeman removed me when Lady Marjorie
sent him word: "Would he remove those people" but I always
came back. The children and their nurses came out for a walk
but I still went on. At last the policeman said he must arrest
me, which he did very gently and politely, calling me 'Madam'.
My companion, who had taken no share in the work, now
roused herself and, taking my arm, said she should "rescue
the prisoner" when the policeman also took her into custody
and, holding one of us each side, we all proceeded to
Marylebone Police Station. In a short time we were taken to
the Police Court in a taxi, the policeman asking my leave to
sit inside as he said it would attract less attention. At 2 o'clock
when the Court returned from lunch our case was taken. Mrs.
C. gave an undertaking to Mr. Plowden to be of good
behaviour and was discharged. Mr. Plowden was facetious to
me; I got three weeks in the 2nd Division and was removed to
a cell to wait for Black Maria, Dr. Patch, getting me lunch and
being very sweet and sympathetic, arriving at Holloway about
7 o'clock.* [2]

This was Sarah's second term of imprisonment but the routines were no
easier to accept than they had been the first time. After a mandatory bath,
which she enjoyed, she was taken to a room where she was ordered to

remove all her clothes. *"How docile we were in those days"* she later said. She was given a short chemise and, although there was a fire in the room, she was still very cold and walked back and forth in the room. Her captors asked her why she could not stand still and she replied: *"You would not, clothed as I am, on a winter night. I am cold."*

She was then told to hold her arms out and was thoroughly searched, including her hair, for concealed contraband. When they were satisfied she was given a set of coarse prison clothes. Finally, she was directed to a huge clothes basket full of old shoes and was told to select a pair. She eventually found a pair which were a reasonable match but her feet became very sore due to nails sticking up in the heels. She showed them to the wardress who brought her a new pair.

> *"Then the dreary routine began again – confinement to one's cell from 11 o'clock, when we came in from our daily hour's exercise, till the next morning at 9.30 when we went to Chapel; then 10 to 11 again exercise and solitary confinement in one's cell all the rest of the time. I could not now have my own books or writing materials and we were expected to work. The long canvas bags with which postmen clear the pillar boxes were brought us and we had to sew the seams with unbleached thread which we made almost black with wax. I never would make more than one a day (two were expected) so some smaller bags were given me; but I could not manage these either and, finally, I was given knitting needles and wool and knitted a large pair of men's socks."* (2)

When she had completed her first week, Sarah noticed that a large number of WSPU members had appeared among them at exercise time and in chapel where all the prisoners sat on low wooden benches without backs. At exercise they were required to walk in single file for one hour and were not permitted to speak. When the wardress came in in the morning to ask, as usual, if she had any 'requisitions', Sarah said yes, she had, she requested to speak to the Visiting Magistrate. The wardress demanded to know the reason and Sarah told her that she intended to request that during the daily exercise, having walked for half an hour in one direction, they should be allowed to turn round and walk the other way. The wardress, possibly relieved that it was nothing more serious, said she thought this could be arranged without bothering the Visiting Magistrate. The next day, to the surprise of everyone except Sarah, this new measure was introduced.

Though she kept her spirits up, the physical strain of prison life was beginning to take its toll and Sarah was feeling very unwell.

> *"The backache by day and the miserable discomfort at night, caused by a mattress so narrow one could hardly balance on it, joined to unnourishing and insufficient food. When I sent for the Doctor he and I knew equally that my symptoms pointed to the need of more food, more rest, more fresh air; the medicine he gave me was no use without these. I said to a wardress: "it is a shame to put women like us who have done no harm in the 2nd Division" and she glanced contemptuously at my dingy brown clothes and said: "you're not in the 2nd Division" and I found that we were in the 3rd Division; but the same afternoon the green serge garments of the 2nd Division were brought us to change into and next day (Monday) when a question was asked in the House about our being in the 3rd Division, Mr. Gladstone was able to say the questioner was misinformed, we were in the 2nd."* [2]

The psychological effects of imprisonment were also having a depressive effect on Sarah's motivating force.

> *"Many of our readers may have seen Holloway from outside and said to themselves that the handsome castle, in a good part of London, could not be a very terrible abode; but these would be overlooking the fact that it is a cell measuring roughly 6 ft 10 ins x 10 ft 6 ins that each of us occupies and that, when the heavy door closes on us, and the key turns in*

The release from Holloway in August 1908 of Mary Leigh and Edith New, members of the WSPU who had served a sentence of two months for having broken two windows of 10 Downing Street.

> the lock, it is little consolation that we are in a fine castle. We
> are in a cell in a wing, the outside walls are lined with cells."
> (2)

When she had completed her three week sentence, Sarah was released on her own as most of her fellow prisoners were serving a full month. A reception committee of WFL members awaited her outside the prison and she complied with their request to make a speech though she was feeling far from well.

Teresa Billington-Greig, one of the Founders of the WFL, was serving as National Honorary Organizing Secretary of the League and in June 1908 she and Sarah Benett were sent as the WFL representatives to the fourth 'Conference of the International Woman Suffrage Alliance' in Amsterdam.

It was a notable event with 21 countries represented. Delegates from all the British suffrage groups were present and the President of the Alliance declared that: *"England is the storm centre of our movement."* It was agreed that the Conference should be held in London the following year.

In the autumn of 1908 Sarah's integrity and organising ability were recognised by the Committee of the Women's Freedom League with her appointment as their Treasurer. For a time after her release from prison she had been working in the peaceful ambience of the League's headquarters at 18 Buckingham Street but did not see eye-to-eye with the Secretary, Teresa Billington-Greig. The continual arguments between the two women was one of the reasons quoted by Maud Arncliffe-Sennet for her resignation from the WFL in 1910. In her autobiography, *'The Child'*, she recorded that Billington-Greig was not popular with members and describes her as a brilliant but weak secretary. Nor did she have a high opinion of Sarah whom she described as a tiresome and quarrelsome woman – which she may very well have been – she was a lady of strong opinions!

Sarah's period at headquarters had enabled her to recover from the malaise she had suffered since her release from prison but when she felt that her health had recovered sufficiently, she became anxious to get back to active duties in the field.

WOMEN'S SOCIAL & POLITICAL UNION POSTCARD

Teresa Billington-Greig, a founder of the WFL and its National Organising Secretary who, with Sarah, represented the League at the Conference of the International Woman Suffrage Alliance in Amsterdam in 1908.

6. "Black Friday"

Friday 18th November 1910

In April 1908 Sir Henry Campbell-Bannerman had resigned as Prime Minister of the Liberal government, due to illness, and had been succeeded by Herbert Asquith who was well known for his strong opposition to women's suffrage. He therefore became the number one target for all women's groups who were determined to put their case to him and attempt to obtain some form of support for their aims. Secondary targets were two of Asquith's principal ministers – David Lloyd George, Chancellor of the Exchequer, and Winston Churchill, President of the Board of Trade, both of whom had previously expressed a degree of support for the women's demands but had become notably silent on the subject since their government had come to power.

There were two principal reasons for their reticence: Churchill, who at one point actually proposed a referendum on women's suffrage, (which was turned down by Asquith), came to realise that the upper- and middle-class property-owning women who were more likely to get the vote with a restricted franchise, and those more likely to use their vote in the improbable event of universal suffrage, would tend to be Tory rather than Liberal supporters and any concession to the suffragists would therefore weaken the Liberal government to the point where it could, in Churchill's words: *"perish like Sisera at a woman's hand"*.

LIBRARY OF CONGRESS – GEORGE GRANTHAM BAIN COLLECTION

The other reason was that both politicians, despite their sympathy for the cause, were beginning to find the tactics of the WSPU and other militant groups tiresome and counter productive. In a 1909 letter to C P Scott, Editor of the *'Manchester Guardian'*, Lloyd George confided:

**Herbert Henry Asquith,
Liberal Prime Minister 1908-1916**

Winston Churchill.   **David Lloyd George.**

"The action of the Militants is ruinous. The feeling amongst sympathisers of the cause in the House [of Commons] is one of panic. I am frankly not very hopeful of success if these tactics are persisted in." [16]

Churchill, whose meetings were continually interrupted by aggressive heckling, gradually lost sympathy with the WSPU and pointed out that, though he had always voted in favour of women's suffrage, the suffragettes' behaviour had seriously weakened his support. Eventually, on an occasion when they had interrupted yet another of his meetings, he declared:

"Nothing would [now] induce me to vote for giving votes to women." [17]

The women's hatred of Asquith was fanned by his arrogance and lack of courtesy towards them. Stories were circulated of his refusal to answer questions at public meetings which were put by women and his failure to reply to letters he received from the women's groups. In 1909 an alleged suffragette plot to assassinate Asquith was thwarted by Scotland Yard and in the same year, in Bristol, Churchill was attacked by a woman with a whip who drove him off the platform into the path of an oncoming train. He was dragged clear by his wife Clementine.

The WFL "Battlebus".

Sarah played her part in this harassment of government ministers:

"Our actions which did not result in imprisonment during 1908/9/10 were many and important. I was always busy taking part in the successful campaign against Winston Churchill at Manchester, and then at Wolverhampton, where I discovered that a woman was on the parliamentary register. I sought her out and persuaded her to record her vote, which she did without opposition.

"I went to Birmingham in the autumn and tried to carry out my instructions to stand at the door of the hall where Asquith was speaking but the town was barricaded against us. I struggled again and again up the side streets, the crowd pushing me on and the police hurling me back, and did not give up the struggle till the meeting was over. I think orders

had been sent down that we were not to be arrested as I had seen my two companions rushed up the street by the police but had met them again in the evening at our hotel." [2]

The Prime Minister's parliamentary constituency was East Fife which he visited whenever he could. But even north of the border he could not escape the attentions of the women's groups:

"In a vigorous campaign against Asquith in East Fife. We were nearly torn to pieces by a huge crowd of liberal politicians, largely mixed with roughs, and were only rescued by friendly men and the police and put in trams, in which we travelled a long way, returning towards evening. I got two work girls to let me walk with them. When we tried to hold a meeting at Leven, outside the Hall where Asquith was speaking, and again in the Market Place at Cupar on polling day, we were nearly all taken into custody but released as soon as Mr. Asquith got away. In the early summer of 1909, we held meetings in every district around Westminster culminating in a deputation from one of these meetings anticipating arrest when another deputation would have followed; but the first deputation being allowed to remain, the picketing of Parliament, all the hours it was in session, began and continued for three months. August 1909 culminated in arrests when we picketed 10 Downing Street." [2]

In July 1909, Marion Wallace Dunlop, having been sentenced to one month's imprisonment for defacing a wall with suffrage slogans, became the first woman to use hunger striking as a means of gaining public attention. The prison authorities, wishing at all costs to avoid creating suffragette martyrs, released her after she had fasted for 91 hours. She had established the precedent and many women followed her example. In September the authorities responded by introducing force feeding. The prisoner would be wrapped in a sheet and bound in a reinforced chair while

Lady Constance Bulwer-Lytton who exposed discrimination in the authorities' choice of prisoners for force feeding.

Marion Wallace Dunlop from Inverness who was the first woman to go on hunger strike in July 1909

the prison doctor inserted a nasal tube and introduced liquid feed. This brutal practice engendered much public sympathy and criticism in the Press.

It also became clear that class discrimination was being exercised by the authorities in deciding which hunger strikers should be released on the grounds of ill health and which should be force fed. Lady Constance Bulwer-Lytton, a committed suffragette, had gone on hunger strike while in Holloway but had been gently treated and avoided forced feeding 'on medical grounds'. In 1910 she was arrested again in Liverpool, this time disguised as a working woman and giving her name as Jane Warton. Without the protection of her social rank she received rough treatment and was duly force fed.

In an article in '*The Vote*' of 25th November 1909, Sarah appealed to WFL members to think carefully before condemning plans drawn up, with great care and forethought, by the Committee. She also urged them to donate generously to the work of the League and to give their full support to the forthcoming Festival at the Albert Hall on 11th December:

> *"The distinction between a militant and a peaceful society is*
> *that the proceedings of the former are necessarily secret: we*
> *cannot reveal our plans to the enemy, and so we must keep*

them from our friends. We may have been elaborating a plan for a couple of years – we may have rejected others we thought almost as good. Then we proceed to work out the details and allot their tasks to our splendid volunteers and the action comes, on friend and foe alike, as a bolt from the blue. I have nothing to say here about the foe, but I should like to suggest to friends that, if they are inclined to find fault they should restrain themselves until they have had time to go through the thought-processes which have led to the plan's adoption. We are duly thankful to those who hail each fresh effort as the finest thing that has been done yet and wait and watch for new heights to be reached, new deeds to be thankful for.

"Lately I heard a clergyman draw attention to the number of things which were crimes now but had not been when he was young. The crimes for which the Women's Freedom League is answerable are of this class. In free England it has never been a crime to ask for liberty, insistently if necessary, backing up one's words with deeds. The march of events has made what used to be a great event, fraught with hopes and possibilities, into a great crime. A general election should give to all who will have to obey the laws the new Parliament will make a chance to choose some Member of that Parliament pledged to champion their interests; whom they will be in a position to control. When we read in the Labour Leader, the Morning Post, the Nation, &c., of the plans and hopes of different parties from the coming struggle we must, I think, be strengthened in our attitude of revolt against our position of outlawry. It is a revolt which must cost us much in both money and service. May I urge those who really cannot give service to keep their enthusiasm alive by giving money freely. I must not enlarge on the point that money is service. The services and enjoyments which parents or relations denied themselves have provided some of you with money, which gives you the power to command services for yourself . . . or the Women's Freedom League. Which shall it be? I think I can assure you

Israel Zangwill, British author of Latvian descent who believed passionately in Jewish emancipation and Women's Suffrage.

it will be both if you spend all you possibly can on the Albert Hall Festival on December 11th. The Women's Pageant or Bernard Shaw's play, or half a dozen other items, should suffice alone to draw a "full house". Then you cannot elsewhere see stars of the magnitude of Ellen Terry, Margaret Halstan, Mrs. Langtry – on one day and for such small sums. And to pass from enjoyments to serious interests, we are to have an address – certainly brilliant and probably full of new and weighty arguments – from Mr. Israel Zangwill; words of wisdom and charm and inspiration from Mrs. Billington-Greig, restored to us after her serious illness; and our President, Mrs. Despard, will be with us." [18]

SARAH BENETT

In November 1910 the first *'Conciliation Bill'*, which would have extended the franchise to around one million women of substance, was axed by the Prime Minister after its second reading on the grounds that, with the general election imminent, there was no more parliamentary time available for it. The WSPU was outraged and its response was instant and emphatic: three hundred women were despatched to demonstrate at Westminster and in the ensuing fracas with police many were brutally manhandled and injured. Emmeline Pankhurst, accompanied by Elizabeth Garrett Anderson and Sophia Duleep Singh, led the deputation and demanded to see the Prime Minister. Though they were allowed through the police cordon, Asquith

WIKIPEDIA – IN PUBLIC DOMAIN

Dr. Elizabeth Garrett Anderson and Mrs. Emmeline Pankhurst on 'Bloody Friday'. Dr. Anderson was the first woman to qualify as a doctor and surgeon and the first female magistrate in Britain.

refused to see them and they were ordered to leave

Some two thirds of the protesters were victims of the heavy-handed tactics and, despite the fact that the police were briefed to *"tire the women out"* and avoid arrests where possible, there were still 129 arrests made as the women tried to force their way into the parliament buildings. These were not the restrained arrests of earlier days – there were many reports of women being beaten on their breasts, having knees thrust between their legs and being thrown against walls and into crowds of hostile, groping men. Much of the violence was of a sexual nature and the incident has been recorded in the history of the Women's Movement as 'Black Friday'.

Despite an appeal to the Press from Winston Churchill not to report the violence or to publish any photographs, several newspapers were so outraged by the behaviour of the police that they reported it in shocking detail. The *'Daily Mirror'* published

WIKIMEDIA COMMONS – IN PUBLIC DOMAIN

Princess Sophia Duleep Singh daughter of Maharajah Duleep Singh and granddaughter of Maharajah Ranjit Singh, 'Lion of the Punjab'.

Photograph of Ada Wright, a victim of heavy-handed policing during 'Black Friday', published on the front page of the *'Daily Mirror'* on Saturday 19th November 1910.

a photograph *(right)* of Ada Wright, a suffragette who had been assaulted by the police, lying on the ground protecting her face with her hands. This, and other publicity adverse to the establishment, hardened public sympathy for the women's cause and anger towards the government.

During the passage of the *Conciliation Bill* the WSPU had suspended militant action but after 'Black Friday' they let it be known that the truce was over and their activities would be intensified.

The moderate reaction of the WFL to the sabotage of the *Conciliation Bill* did not meet with Sarah's approval and she felt the time had come to return to the WSPU which, despite the fact that it was under the autocratic control of the Pankhursts, was the only organisation which appeared to be taking positive action:

> *"I had suffered much and worked hard for the cause but my real militancy did not begin till the autumn of 1910 when Asquith and the Speaker played the farce of pretending they had discovered something about a women's amendment to the 'Suffrage Bill', a Bill which no-one had ever wanted and which was therefore slaughtered without any demur except from the women. I had been working with the W.F.L. till then but I could*

124

not assent to the very moderate tone of their protest. I shared the furious indignation of the great body of members of the W.S.P.U. and, consequently, having listened unmoved to arguments for this continuance of the 'Truce' at a meeting at Caxton Hall of the W.F.L., I determined to find expression for my convictions through the machinery of the W.S.P.U. Late in the afternoon of Friday 18th November, I found my way to Caxton Hall and sent my name up to the platform as a volunteer. From about 3 o'clock, groups of, I think, eleven women left the Hall and I went out with one of these groups with a handsome badge 'Deputation 1910' pinned on my coat, and with a roll of paper containing a Petition to present to the House." [2]

Sarah avoided arrest on 'Black Friday' but she played her part in the battle with the police and was not without minor injuries as a result:

"We tramped along in the semi-darkness till we were near the railings of Westminster Abbey; then immediately the group faded away and we were a struggling unit in a jeering dangerous crowd. The Choirboys from the Abbey were making fun of us inside the railings and, outside, we soon found ourselves up against a crowd of police with linked arms and I heard one say as he drove us back: "It reminds me of my football days". I fancy every one of us had the same hopeless fight and suffered more or less severely – I knocked off one or two helmets and was marked down for vengeance by a truculent looking constable. He seized both my arms pinching one till the flesh was black and blue and giving a savage twist to the other which would, I think, have broken it had I not involuntarily ducked to escape the pain he was inflicting. After this, I returned to Caxton Hall feeling that for this time I could do no more." [2]

Kenneth Duke Scott and his wife Alice (née Henderson), ardent suffragists who later emigrated to the USA where they continued the battle for women's rights.

ERIC DUKE SCOTT

In January 1910 Lloyd George, who was the Chancellor of the Exchequer at the time, was to address a meeting in Reading. During the previous night, two young suffragettes from London hid themselves in the tight space below the speakers' platform where they waited in extreme discomfort, without food or water, for 17 hours until the appropriate point of the Chancellor's speech when they emerged in front of him and accused him of robbery for taking taxes from women who had no vote.

After the meeting, a 'tall and powerful man', was to show that it was not only women who were forcing their attention on to government ministers. Grabbing Lloyd George by his lapels, he would not allow him to proceed until he had listened to what he had to say. The man was 27 year-old Kenneth Duke Scott, an agricultural scientist who, together with his wife, were ardent suffragists and, although he was pulled off the Chancellor by the crowd, he explained his actions and made his points in a long and impassioned letter to the *'Berkshire Chronicle'* of 8th January 1910 which the editor thought was worth printing in full and which is reproduced at the end of this chapter.

The injuries sustained by the suffragettes on 'Black Friday' had taught them that they must protect themselves more effectively when they were likely to come up against the police:

> *"The following Tuesday, 22nd November 1910, we again gathered at Caxton Hall and speeches were made till word was brought that the House had risen . . . Then again we sallied*

forth, but this time we hurried anyhow to Downing Street to show our wrath against Asquith. Most of us were well protected round our bodies and arms with cotton wool and corrugated cardboard bound on with coarse muslin. It made a comfortable armour and would certainly have prevented a repetition of the experiences of Black Friday. I got through and was very near No. 10. I kept my footing and helped myself forward by holding on to the leather belts of policemen who were engaged with half a dozen other suffragettes. I rather think Inspector Wells, who knew me well, saw that I was in a perilous position and gave a signal to a man to arrest me, which they did, taking me through to Charles Street. Here we met a fresh detachment of police with a sergeant at their head and my captors said in an agitated under tone: "Make haste, they're nearly there". I laughed remembering that 'they' were unarmed women but the sergeant without a smile turned to his men and gave the word: "Double" and they all set off at a sharp trot. I was charged with obstruction; we were all bailed as usual and appeared next morning at Bow Street before Sir A. de Rutzen who was very much incensed because he had received orders to discharge all of us who had not committed any acts of violence. He said he had never been so insulted and that it was equally unjust to him and the accused. However, I was taken into the Court and at once told that I was discharged. My twisted arm continued swollen and painful and I had it massaged for 3 weeks or so, early in the new year." [2]

The following year, 1911, was to see no easing off of pressure from the suffragettes to advance their cause.

Letter from Mr. Kenneth Duke Scott
to the Editor of the *'Berkshire Chronicle'*
published in the edition of 8th January 1910

"SIR – As the perpetrator of Saturday night's assault on Mr. Lloyd George will you allow me to endeavour to clear away some of the fog that has arisen around my act. You will I trust admit that odds of 6,000 to one are great enough to face without anything by way of exaggeration and misleading statements. Such varied accounts of what I did have reached my ears that I shall be much obliged to you if you will permit me to say what I did and why I did it. I have been variously accused of intent to "stab", "hit on the jaw" and "throttle" Mr. Lloyd George.

One good "brother" connected with a movement with which I am connected too has spread the report that I shook Mr. Lloyd George violently which is, of course, untrue. When I found myself in the local Press reserve I knew that I had dropped into a position of exceptional opportunity to remind the Chancellor of the claims of women. If I had wanted to do any of the acts imputed to me do you think, sir, I should have patiently endured two mortal hours of suspense previous to the act being done? I could have effectually prevented the speech by breaking his jaw before the meeting but I should also have upset any possibility of our cause becoming popular in Reading and besides I am not a lover of violence and would repudiate any suggestion of such an act. As the Chancellor came down the steps I gave a reporter a note containing the question I wished to ask Mr. Lloyd George. I then stepped in front of him and took him by the lapels of his overcoat to attract his attention and I asked him why he neglected to consider and speak about votes for women. He raised his eyebrows and said distinctly "How can I?" He then wheeled around and backed away from me. As I had more to say I held on and a pack of hysterical stewards and successful people from the platform ended our conversation somewhat abruptly. Mr. Rufus Isaacs pacified my captors and to him I herewith tender my thanks. What I did was, of course, part of a concerted plan to repeatedly remind Liberals in general and Mr. Lloyd George in particular that all the talk of this year becoming a year of grace because the people asserted their right to self government with unmistakable emphasis is sheer hypocrisy when one considers that the man who said that has asserted his belief in women's enfranchisement.

It seems clear that street barriers, extra police, detectives and a system of application forms or tickets and all the rest of the additional expense and trouble are really not worthwhile when, with comparatively little trouble, we are always able to bring the demand for consideration forward. The fact that the two women evaded a search party under the platform and that one of my comrades was thrown out twice and nearly succeeded in getting in a third time seems to me to show very clearly that no organization is of any avail to checkmate our actions and the organizers might just as well give in and have done with it. You can't outwit a suffragette.

There are however a few arguments that have been put to me since that may have occurred to other people as well. The first is that our actions are ill-timed, unseemly and hysterical and that it is not fair to pester a man in such a way. To answer this objection it is necessary to hark back to the beginning of the "hot time". When Christabel Pankhurst and Annie Kenney first asked Sir Edward Grey a reasonable question at the proper time and by giving notice of it on paper they were refused an answer thrown out of the meeting with much violence, for persisting in demanding an answer and arrested for protesting to the public outside the hall. For a dozen or so meetings this was repeated, and the course was then decided upon of putting their questions at any time during the meeting and of heckling the ministers until they gave women proper consideration. This led to the historic utterance of Lloyd George: "Let them be ruthlessly flung out." Times have changed since then, the crowd on Saturday, we are told, protested against the ill-usage of one of the women as she was being ejected. The Press of the country, too, has reported the incident as an assault upon a suffragist. I do not expect you, Sir, to print the tales of fury and devilish outrage that have been committed upon sincere and high principled women as they were being ejected from meetings in the past. But let us put all cant aside and remember that no suffragist can be expected to reverence the person of a cabinet minister when he has been guilty of causing outrages of various kinds to be committed upon the persons of pure and earnest women. As to hysteria I would suggest to a man making such a complaint "You just take it on". Go and lie all night under the floor of the carsheds on your back and on the stone setts with just sufficient space to get in and none to move about and suffer cold and hunger and every possible inconvenience for 12 or 18 hours or so add to that the nervousness and suspense of a life time gone through during those hours and then say such a soul that comes through that ordeal is suffering from hysteria. This is a time when the nailing

down on the lid of the coffin of the anti-suffragist might well be completed and I have here, Sir, four nails that I should like to drive home.

"Women" it is said, "do not want the vote." That reminds me of an old landlady who never provided supper for her lodgers because if she took any it always gave her indigestion. In well ordered households supper is provided whether all partake or not. A housewife who refused it on the ground that all did not want it would be universally looked upon as a stingy mean old cat. **Nail number one.**

It is said that "the vote is no use." Ask the gentlemen of Wargrave who possess a vote for a town house, a vote for a country house and a vote for a boathouse whether they find the vote any use. If they make no reply offer to take away their boathouse vote, then watch the dust rise. Because men make no satisfactory use of their votes, after having done far greater crimes than the Suffragettes to obtain them, is no argument against women being recognised as citizens. The women who want the vote are different from the women who do not want the vote. The Suffragette knows that the sex life of our civilisation is in a disgusting mess. She knows further that our industrial and economic life is also in a mess, and she has found out that our prison system is also in a mess and further that our party politics have nothing much to do with politics properly so-called – the science of the Polis or State. Party politics are in a mess. The Anti-Suffragette pretends she does not or actually does not know that these things need readjustment. The one is educated the other is ignorant. **Nail number two.**

Perhaps you think, Sir, that I presume too much when I regard the Anti-Suffragettes as dead, but consider how little we have heard of her this winter. Where can she be?

Ah I have a clue. She has found, Sir, . . . been home at any late for a fortnight and at this moment throughout England and, our thousands of these good ladies are neglecting their homes, their children and their husbands touting for votes to be given to their respective parties. We, Sir, believe that it would be more wholesome for women to stay in the home, and if necessary be canvassed and straightforwardly vote, and use their influence openly and above board besides it would only take a minute for them to vote compared with the hours they are now spending touting. **Nail number three.**

Finally, there is the notion that there is nothing in the Suffrage agitation. I can only state that this movement will mark an era in our civilisation. Brand the Suffragette as a criminal if you like. Give her 2nd and 3rd class prison treatment if you will. You only show your processes of justice to be worse than those of Russia, where political prisoners are treated as politicals. Jameson, the promoter of the "Boer War Ltd." got 18 months as a political. If acquiescence in things as they are is to be the mark of respectability, then the only place left for an honest man or woman is the prison. This is nothing new,

of course. Class her as a criminal lunatic, and you do but bracket the Suffragette as equal top of the school of humanity: equal top with the greatest teachers, heroes and discoverers whose monuments we build, whilst giving the fiery cross to their modern representatives. The appeal of the Suffragette is a great human appeal. It is the appeal of woman, and its efforts are felt, and will be felt, from the highest Divine Immanence in man's soul to the lowest most brutal manifestation of human character. There is no soul so utterly devoid of beauty and devotion as to be untouched at some time by the appeal of woman, be it that of mother, sister, lover or wife. If the Anti-Suffragists are outside this sphere of influence God help them. If I have shown by these few words that there is something in it and something worth fighting for then I would point out that there is still an infinite unspoken and as yet unmanifest. Nothing else matters.

Kenneth D. Scott
Hurst, Twyford, Berkshire

P.S. If people object to militant tactics I would refer them to the Suffrage shop in the Market Place run by the constitutional. The most important committee rooms in town – K.D.S.

7. War on Windows

Hampstead, 2nd April 1911

Having moved permanently to London, Sarah had disposed of her house in Burslem and was now living at 25 Ferncroft Avenue, Hampstead, a substantial house in a prosperous suburb from where she was well placed to continue her militant activities in the capital.

As the 1911 National Census approached, several women's groups urged their members to boycott it and refuse to provide information to the enumerators in protest against women's exclusion from the franchise. If the government did not consider women to be full citizens, they argued, their existence was not significant and should not be recorded.

Many women simply refused to give details, others defaced the Census forms with *"Votes for Women"* and other apt slogans. Sarah returned a blank, uncompleted schedule in a plain envelope addressed to the enumerator with the following statement:

"I am denied the full rights of citizenship, so I will not perform the duties of a citizen. I will not help to supply with information a government which classes me with criminals and lunatics and I refuse therefore to answer the Census questions"

25 Ferncroft Avenue, Sarah's house in Hampstead.

ADRIAN PILLING

131

'Mouse Castle', 2 Campden Hill Square, where Census evaders took refuge on 2nd April 1911.

ELIZABETH CRAWFORD

Other women boycotted the Census by 'disappearing' on the Census night. The house of the Brackenbury family in Campden Hill Square, Kensington, known to suffragettes as 'Mouse Castle', became a refuge for some 25 evaders on Census night. Groups of friends organised 'sleep ins' so the maximum number of women would be absent from their homes and untraceable on the night.

Emily Wilding Davison, who would later make headlines by throwing herself under the King's horse in the Derby, hid during Census night in a cupboard in the Chapel of St. Mary Undercroft in the Palace of Westminster so she could legitimately claim her residence as 'The House of Commons'. She is recorded in the Census as having been *"found hiding in the crypt"*.

In May 1911 the second *Conciliation Bill* was debated and was passed with a significant majority. However, Asquith proposed alternative legislation for universal male suffrage and the Bill was dropped later in the year.

The following month Sarah took part in the Great Coronation Procession to the Albert Hall organised by the WSPU to demonstrate their loyalty to the new King George V, who was to be crowned the following week, and in the hope of soliciting his support for their cause. The event was promoted by them as *"The greatest procession of women since the world began."*

Emily Wilding Davison who hid in a cupboard in the Palace of Westminster on Census Night 1911 so she could give her address as "The House of Commons". Later she achieved everlasting fame as the woman who was killed throwing herself at the king's horse in the Derby.

Welsh suffragists in London for the Coronation Procession.

On the afternoon of 17th June 1911, 40,000 women assembled at the Westminster end of the Victoria Embankment and, at 5.30 pm, set off, five abreast for the Albert Hall. The marching column was five miles long and the front had reached its destination before the rear had been marshalled at the start. The marchers were accompanied by 100 bands and it was reported in *The Globe* that a feature of the demonstration was a series of tableaux depicting important events which had been influenced by women; these were performed largely by actresses who were well represented among the marchers. The meeting at the Albert Hall was conducted by Emmeline Pankhurst and another WSPU meeting was held at the same time in Kensington Town Hall.

In late November and early December 1911 there were further large-scale WSPU demonstrations resulting in Sarah's third arrest on 13th December. She was released on 13th February 1912 but it was not long before she was in trouble again. WSPU tactics had hardened and now included the smashing of shop windows so Sarah bought herself a toffee hammer, the recommended tool for the job, and was ready for action.

Rebel with a Cause

"*I had now given myself entirely to militancy; my family were estranged from me and I had no interests or occupations beyond the struggle in which I was taking part. I had nearly settled on my course of action when I went to see someone on whom I depended to make things a little clearer to me and, after seeing her, I decided on immediate action. This was about 12 o'clock on Friday 1st March just seventeen days after my release. I ran home and then to my Club where I made final preparations and, just before 6 o'clock, I sauntered into Regent Street which was thronged with the usual crowd of listless nobodies and I thought that, somehow or other, everyone else was shirking and I never could call their attention to myself; but I was heartened up by the crash of falling glass on the other side of the street. The first of my three shops was a jewellers and it would have been simplest and safest to smash the large centre window, but it was getting dusk and it was not possible for me to risk the looting of his stock of watches and ornaments. So, instead, I used my hammer to break the smaller window close to the door and I think he saw me do it. I moved quickly on and broke the window of a tailor next door and was immediately seized by a man from each of the shops who handed me over to an inspector in plain clothes, who was so absorbed in giving me a fatherly lecture on the error of my ways as he conducted me to Vine Street Police Station, that I was able with my free hand to loosen the bow of a piece of black braid, which went over one shoulder, and from which depended a black serge bag in which was my hammer. It fell heavily to the ground under the archway in Swallow Street; I heard the clatter but my captor did not as, a little later, he asked me to give him my hammer. Of course I refused and he consoled himself by saying it would be found when I was searched but, of course, I knew better and later I chaffed a matron for her inability to find it. There were friends at all the*

Police Stations and I was bailed and went home. The whole of next day was spent at Bow Street with such a crowd of fellow captives that my head ached with their chatter. We had come to the conclusion that we would not take bail and we were all taken to Holloway when the Court rose and I remained there, on remand, for nearly a week. I was taken to Bow Street again on the 8th March and, as I was suffering from tooth ache, I asked those who had come in to be helpful to bail me and two ladies readily consented to do this. I was at my dentist's at 9 o'clock next morning and at Bow Street about 10. My case was not heard until just before the Court rose; I think I was very nearly the last suffragette Sir Curtis Bennett tried. I made some sort of feeble defence and I think he took a malicious pleasure in calling me Bennett and arranging that, although the charge had been so arranged that it could be summarily dealt with, I should not on that account escape lightly. I was given two months for one window and one month for the other, the sentences to run consecutively, and a visible pang passed through the group of friends who were waiting for our return from the Court when I told them that I had three months hard labour. [2]

Five days later, George Lansbury, Labour MP for Bow and Bromley and a fervent supporter of the WSPU, questioned the Home Secretary on the apparently artbitrary handing out of sentences of hard labour to suffragettes. He asked:

George Lansbury, close friend of the Pankhursts and ardent supporter of women's rights. He eventually became leader of the Labour Party in the 1930s.

New No. 607.
Old No. 114.

METROPOLITAN POLICE.

_W_ Division.

Cannon Row Station.

Take Notice, that you _Sarah Bennett_

are bound in the sum of _Two_ Pounds to

appear at the _Bow Street_ Police Court, situated at

Bow Street at _ten_

o'clock _A._M., on the _22nd_ day of _November_

191_1_ , to answer the charge of*

Committing malicious damage

and unless you then appear there, further proceedings will be taken.

Dated this _21st_ day of _November_

One Thousand Nine Hundred and _Eleven_

Crocker Insp.

Officer on Duty.

* Being found drunk in a public street, or being guilty, while drunk, of disorderly behaviour in a street or whatever the charge may be.

25 00 | 4 | 10   50000-9-10.   M.P   81B

> " . . . *if the London magistrates were advised by the Home Office or police authorities to sentence the prisoners connected with the recent suffrage disturbances to sentences of hard labour and not to discriminate between first and second offenders; and, if so, will the Home Secretary review the sentences, so as to apportion the punishment of these offenders in accordance with their individual guilt?"* [19]

The Home Secretary, Reginald McKenna, replied:

> *"The answer to the first part of the question is in the negative. With regard to the second, I can only say that no case has been made out sufficient, in my opinion, to justify interference by means of the Prerogative of Mercy with any of the sentences passed on these offenders."* [19]

On 28th March 1912, while Sarah was serving her sentence in Holloway, the third *Conciliation Bill, The Parliamentary Franchise (Women) Bill* was defeated by 222 votes to 208. A major factor in this result was the fears of the Irish Parliamentary Party, which controlled 84 seats at Westminster, that

GEORGE GRANTHAM BAIN COLLECTION, LIBRARY OF CONGRESS

a debate on women's suffrage might delay and thwart the upcoming Bill for Irish Home Rule. However, this did not stop the anti-suffrage elements of press and public from attributing the defeat to the suffragettes' militant tactics. They were particularly outraged by the fact that the WSPU had escalated their violent tactics at the same time as a national miners' strike

**Reginald McKenna,
Home Secretary 1911-1915.**

was already injuring the country. The '*Pall Mall Gazette*' of Friday 29th March 1912 reported on the *Conciliation Bill:*

> "*Last year that measure received its second reading by a majority of 167. Last night it was rejected by 14 votes – 222 to 208. This is the answer of Parliament to the window smashing. The real feeling of the House seems to have been very imperfectly expressed by the figures. When the result was disclosed there was a scene of tremendous enthusiasm – the kind of enthusiasm that rarely occurs save when a government is defeated. Hats were thrown in the air, handkerchiefs were waved and for a few minutes the House surrendered itself to a perfect storm of delight . . . members had realised the depth of public indignation at the outrages of the suffragettes and the perils of refusing to make a firm stand against violence. The intrusion of the window smashers upon a national crisis of such gravity as the coal strike has given the measure of suffragette mind and morals, and sent all waverers to the side of opposition.*" [20]

The Pankhursts were furious about this latest setback as they had received intimations of support for the Bill from eight government ministers who had then changed their minds at the last minute. Emmeline Pankhurst joined Sarah in Holloway for a two-month sentence for her part in the window breaking. Her daughter, Christabel, who was even more militant than her mother, was wanted by the police for '*Conspiracy, Procuring, Aiding and Abetting persons to commit offences under Section 51 of the Malicious Damage to Property Act*' and fled into exile in Paris from where she made plans for even more violent action including arson of public buildings and the houses of government ministers.

However, elements of the membership, led by Mr. and Mrs. Pethick-Lawrence, who had been the Union's staunchest supporters from the earliest days, were becoming uneasy about the escalating violence which they felt would lose them the support of the public and of their own members. The

Mrs. Emmeline Pankhurst in prison.

Pethick-Lawrences tried to dissuade Christabel and her mother from the arson campaign. Emmeline Pethick-Lawrence later wrote:

"Mrs. Pankhurst met us with the announcement that she and Christabel had deter-mined upon a new kind of campaign. Henceforward she said there was to be a wide-spread attack upon public and private property . . . They were wrong in supposing that a more revolutionary form of militancy, with attacks dir-ected more and more on the property of individuals, would strengthen the movement and bring it to more speedy victory."
(21)

The interference of the Pethick-Lawrences was deeply resented by the Pankhursts who exercised their autocratic rule by expelling them both from the Union in spite of what they had contributed to its success.

Sarah had by now become an 'old hand' in Holloway; she knew the routines and how to bend many of them to suit her purpose. She recorded that her three month hard labour sentence:

". . . meant that I might only exercise once a day, that I might not have any food sent in and that I might have only educational books to read. However, the Doctor can get round anything and he soon ordered exercise twice a day, as necessary for my health. The great number of prisoners were

late getting to Holloway and then a certain routine had to be gone through with each of them and, before I was done with and locked into my cell, it was 3 o'clock on Sunday morning. I was dead tired and resolved to stay in bed till dinner time next day. I thus escaped (quite involuntarily) a sort of riot among the other prisoners because Mrs. Pankhurst had not been allowed to join them at exercise or Chapel. It was a wet morning and the exercise was in the Wing instead of outside. E.S., one of the 20 who had been with me last time, considerately lifted the flap which covered the little window in my door so that with my eye close against it I could see a good deal. The tumult went on all the time; the wardresses were capturing the prisoners and putting them one by one back in their cells and, for an hour or two after, there was a ceaseless din which was perhaps more trying to us than to the officials, who were not obliged to remain in the Wing after they had us safely locked in. I think we triumphed; at any rate, Mrs. Pankhurst did exercise regularly with the rest of us after that. There were lots of young and active women amongst us and I got hold of some of the young girls (remembering our athletic games before) and began racing and playing rounders and it 'caught on' so that we had regular sports every morning at exercise, some of the women being quite up to a professional standard. Associated labour had been introduced, which meant that any of us who consented to do needlework (this

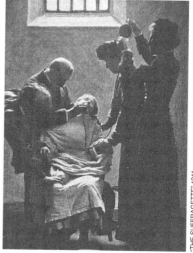

A suffragette on hunger strike being force fed through a nasal tube.

'THE SUFFRAGETTE' 1911

WSPU Medal with "Fed by Force" clasp awarded to Mabel Capper, one of the first hunger strikers to be force fed.

counted for 'hard labour') might sit with the others in the corridor outside their cells, instead of being locked in their cells as soon as exercise was over so that, except for the dinner hour, they were hardly in their cells between 10 and 5 and had only too many opportunities for talk. I, however, on principle, refused to do any labour at all. They tried to induce me to by pinning a card to my door and giving me marks every day, which would have meant a shortening of my sentence, but I did not yield and so they took the card away. I was only allowed educational books; I suppose the prison commissioners thought we were having too easy a time and they made several alterations in the direction of strictness. The only one that I remember was that food might not be sent in to us any time, but only once a week, and then it must not exceed 11 lbs. in weight. This was the signal for a hunger strike; we had a great many discussions and got in touch with the prisoners in D. Wing and all agreed to start at the same time but secretly, and on the first day, the Doctor came into my cell before the dinner things had been removed and looked with satisfaction at my mug which had had a pint of milk in it, but was empty. I did not tell him that I had poured the milk down the sink or that, if he went outside, he would see any of the solid food which the pigeons had not devoured. Next morning we compared notes and I for one felt as well as possible; one's body seemed to have become all spirit. Towards evening however the Doctor knew what was going on and came to me with the direct question: "how long have you been without food?" I said pleasantly: "I had breakfast yesterday morning." He felt my pulse and looked anxious. The next morning when we met for exercise, we were all decidedly unsteady on our legs and our voices had taken on a fractious tone, no part of us seemed quite under our control. I collapsed rapidly, partly because I had been living for six weeks on prison food. The others had been kind in smuggling in food for me, but the supply had not been regular or sufficient. I had observed, when I came out of my cell on the afternoon of the 18th April, preparations for forcible feeding and I was bracing myself to resist it to the last but, instead, the Doctor examined me about 8 o'clock; he found my tongue quite white and my pulse nil. Directly he left me, a wardress came and said I was to go home at once. I went round to the doors of a few cells and told my fellow prisoners, and took some Brand's beef essence and milk. I was helped to get my things together and some one carried them to the door where I found a taxi and a nice girl in nurse's dress and armed with a flask of brandy in case I should collapse; but the fresh air and the excitement of being free braced me up and I did not feel the least ill till next day. In three days I struggled up and went to the Office, as I had been charged, with several messages but I found difficulty in getting anyone to attend to me and the person who at last talked to me treated me very much as if I were an undesirable kitchen maid in want of a place, until she grasped the situation and then she was flattering which was as objectionable. [2]

A typical example of the type of abusive material which was circulated by the anti-suffragists.

We Want the Vote

"HISTORY OF FEMINISM"

From the summer of 1912 the arson attacks planned by Christabel Pankhurst from her exile in Paris began to be implemented. The attacks varied widely from the destruction of mail in pillar boxes, either by fire or by acid squirted through the posting slot, to the burning with acid of slogans on golf greens and destruction of golf clubhouses and cricket pavilions. More seriously, suffragettes were involved in attacks upon railway stations, hotels, country houses and many places of public entertainment such as racecourses. Arrests, hunger strikes and force feeding increased as the year progressed.

Mr. Asquith had for long been guarded by the police against attacks by suffragettes and with the increased violent activity of the WSPU protection was now extended to other senior Cabinet Ministers, in particular Lloyd George, Churchill and McKenna. When they left home in the morning they were accompanied by plain-clothes officers and again in the evening on their journey home.

> "If the Minister walks, the police guard walks; if he leaves in a motor-car they either ride in the car or follow closely in a taxi-cab. In the last named case, the officers – who of course know the Minister's destination – proceed ahead and are ready on the pavement to guard him as he alights." [22]

The houses of the Prime Minister and Chancellor of the Exchequer in Downing Street, of the Home Secretary in Old Queen Street and the First

Lord of the Admiralty in Eccleston Square were guarded round the clock by relays of uniformed police and, for the protection of other Ministers and MPs, police beats in Westminster were shortened so that an officer would never be far away in the event of an incident.

Throughout the summer of 1912 WSPU members lost no opportunity to disrupt government events and to importune the Prime Minister and his cabinet members. On Friday 14th June an official reception was being held at the India Office and a large number of guests stood in line waiting for their introduction to Mr. Asquith. An 'elaborately dressed' lady of about 30 was announced and the Prime Minister extended his hand to her but, instead of taking it, she grabbed the epaulette of his official coat and attempted to wrench it off. No sooner had she been ejected than 'a pale-faced youth of about 20' took hold of the PM by his arms and shouted abuse in his face. He, too, was ejected and was immediately followed by a very well-dressed young woman who seized the Premier by one arm and beat him over the head with her fan. The stewards had great difficulty in extracting him from the woman's clutches. The '*Pall Mall Gazette*' the following day reported that, perhaps understandably:

> "Mr. Asquith was much perturbed at the moment and expressed himself in very forcible terms." [23]

Following this fracas, on Monday 1st July, the Political Committee of the National Liberal Club decided at an emergency meeting that the reception for the Prime Minister which was to take place that Friday should be postponed until the autumn. A great many women had purchased tickets and the committee feared that the WSPU was planning an attack similar to that at Lady Glenconner's recent reception. Lady Glenconner, in common with many other leading society and political hostesses, was a member of 'the Women's National Anti-Suffrage League' (WNASL) which had been founded four years previously with Lady Jersey as its first chairman. At the reception, four women had thrown themselves simultaneously at the Prime Minister and one of the guests who rushed to his assistance had received a very severe bite on his arm from one of the women.

Suffragettes outside the Bow Street Court.

Sarah still believed that violent action was the only way to achieve their aims and, although her age (she was now over 60) restricted her from taking part in the most violent forms of protest, she was still ready to play her part in less physical activities, such as window breaking, and was certainly prepared for further arrests and prison sentences. She later recorded her contempt for women whose contribution was an endless round of public speaking undertaken largely, she believed, to gain personal prestige, and her admiration for those who inspired others by their willingness to endure danger and discomfort for the cause.

> *"Have done every sort of thing; there were two points of view –*
> *we were unconvincing as long as we did pleasant things and*
> *those who had the power to give or withhold the vote never*
> *listened to us, or were absolutely indifferent as long as we did*
> *not inconvenience them. There was another reason against our*

doing pleasant things only – the danger of becoming insincere; can we not all point to women who have got into the habit of platform speaking whenever there is prominent work of that sort to be done? You are sure to see their names and to have the opportunity of hearing them speak of things which they never intend to do; they are enormously diligent in pursuing their object, but it is that they should be heard speaking. I don't know whether they deceive themselves; they do, unfortunately, often deceive others and are a great hindrance to any movement.

"How often I have wanted to say from a platform: "Be ready to throw stones at us up here, be ready to take our places and then cede them to others. Do not make a fetish of names. Make us go out into the bye ways where we can again hear the wail of the suffering instead of applause at our own cheap cleverness.

"It is Lady Constance Lytton and Emily Davison who gave life to our demand not those who, week after week, addressed packed, applauding audiences." [2]

WE WILL HAVE IT!"

8. The Edinburgh March

Charlotte Square, Edinburgh, 12th October 1912

Florence Gertrude Sparagnapane de Fonblanque was born in Leyton in 1864, the daughter of Gaudente Sparagnapane, a wholesale confectioner of Swiss origin, and his wife Aurelia. Florence and her elder sister, Maud, were of striking appearance and both became actresses in which profession they achieved some note in their youth.

In 1891 Florence married a fellow actor, Robert E. Degrenier de Fonblanque, Marquise de Juliers and Comte de Fonblanque. The age on her marriage certificate is given as 22 though she was, in fact, 27. As a married woman she became interested in women's suffrage and, like Sarah Benett, was originally a member of the WSPU before transfering to the WFL after the split. Her sister, Maud, married Henry Robert Arncliffe Sennett, a manufacturer of Christmas crackers and wedding cake ornaments, in 1898. She, too, became a prominent suffragist moving, like her sister and Sarah, from WSPU to WFL and then back again.

In 1912 Florence had the idea of a march, originally to and from Edinburgh, to publicise women's suffrage. The final plan was for a

Maud Arncliffe-Sennett, sister of Florence de Fonblanque, who joined the marchers at Easingwold, Yorkshire.

The six women who completed the full 400 miles from Edinburgh to London. From left: – White, – Brown, Margaret Byham, Florence de Fonblanque, Sarah Benett and – Robinson.

one-way journey from Edinburgh to London with the object of holding meetings and collecting signatures to a petition as they marched south. The petition, requesting the government to introduce a Bill for women's suffrage during the current session, was to be handed to the Prime Minister on their arrival in London. The march had the support of both WSPU and WFL. Sarah, though now aged 62, determined to be part of the scheme:

"Before long, I was attracted by Mrs. de Fonblanque's splendid idea of a march to and from Edinburgh for teaching and getting signatures to a petition. Coming after so much

militancy, we felt it was a reminder that we were always anxious to be peaceable, if it was any use, and that peaceful action between whiles gave point to our bursts of furious militancy when any specially callous act of betrayal was indulged in by the Government. Mrs. de Fonblanque worked out her plan with great pluck and perseverance. It became a march from Edinburgh to London and there were six of us who marched the whole 400 miles and formed the backbone of the undertaking. [2]

The women assembled on Saturday 12th October 1912 in Charlotte Square, Edinburgh, where a huge crowd had gathered for the start. From here they marched the length of Princes Street where around 10,000 spectators lined the route to see them pass. The six 'full-time' ladies led the procession wearing brown woollen suits with bright, emerald green ribbons and rosettes and brown felt hats with green cockades. Between 200 and 300 marchers followed behind to complete the first phase.

"We had a magnificent send off from Edinburgh on 12th October 1912, such a crowd had not been seen since the send off of the Black Watch to the Boer War . . ." [2]

After three miles they reached Portobello where they were served with tea at the Marine Theatre before continuing the march to Musselburgh where they stayed on Sunday before leaving for Headington on Monday morning. As they progressed south, averaging about 11 or 12 miles each day, they would be joined by supporters who would accompany them to the next stop so the 'full-timers' were never without an enthusiastic crowd behind them. At each stop they would hold meetings and solicit signatures for their petition,

One of the women who joined the march in Scotland was Isabel Cowe from St. Abb's in Berwickshire. She had been born in 1868 the youngest of eight children in a family of east coast fishermen. Isabel had been brought up tough and earlier in the year, on 25th July, had been involved in the rescue of passengers from the ss *Glanmire* an iron steamship which had foundered off St. Abb's Head on a voyage from Amsterdam to Grangemouth with general cargo. For her part in the rescue, Isabel had been awarded the 'Royal National Lifeboat Institution's' Gold Brooch for Bravery. She brought her bicycle with her on the march:

> *"Miss Cowe has done splendid work en route, for the bicycle has enabled her to reach many out of the way farm-places and hamlets for signatures and then rejoin the party."* [24]

Foul weather was no impediment to her drive to obtain signatures for the petition and her figure, carrying a hurricane lamp and clad in oilskins and sou'wester, became a familiar sight after meetings. Two years later she was to make headline news again when she refused to pay her Parish Rates and barricaded herself in her house with a hatchet to repel the bailliffs.

> *"We were joined at Easingwold in Yorkshire by Mrs. Arncliffe Sennett (Mrs. de Fonblanque's sister) and had a brilliant indoor meeting; but our meetings were generally in the largest square of each town and, very often, two were held at the same time. People admired our grit as well as our arguments and we got an enormous number of signatures to our petition."* [2]

No effort was spared to obtain signatures. On 4th November the marchers arrived at Newark, in Nottinghamshire, and came upon a group of men repairing telephone cables. Several of the men signed the petition but one man working at the top of a pole said he was not coming down to do it. Ada Wright, the suffragette who had appeared lying on the ground in the famous '*Daily Mirror*' picture of Black Friday, called up to him: *"Will you sign if I bring it up?"* The man agreed and Ada, in heavy ankle-length skirt, climbed the pole and obtained his signature.

Opposite: **The Edinburgh marchers on their arrival in London led by Florence de Fonblanque with Sarah in the second rank holding the forward right-hand side steadying rope for the banner.**

At most of their stops the marchers attracted sizeable crowds which were prepared to listen to them and offer good natured support:

> *". . . and, except that in one or two places we met with fierce opposition, we excited sympathetic interest and a good deal of enthusiasm from first to last."* [2]

One place where they encountered hostility was Peterborough which they reached on Friday 8th November. As the march approached the town they were joined by a group of jeering students who marched behind them singing abusive songs. Later they attempted to hold a meeting in the Stanley Recreation Ground but they were broken up by a hostile crowd shouting, jostling them and letting off fireworks. However, this level of hostility was unusual.

The march continued now covering between 15 and 25 miles a day depending on weather and the number of people who they stopped and talked to on the way. The further south they got the less understanding for their cause they found; the most common reason for people's refusal to sign the petition was disapproval of the window-smashing activities.

On 14th November they reached Hitchin in Hertfordshire and '*The Globe*' reported that only one marcher had to have her shoes resoled though they had covered 393 miles often on rough and wet surfaces. A fine testimonial for the British shoemaking industry.

Finally, on 16th November 1912, the women's triumphant entry into London was reported:

> *"Much interest was evinced in the march of the suffragettes when on Saturday they passed through Finchley from Edinburgh on their walk to London in order to present a monster petition to the Prime Minister urging the Government to give votes for women this session. The ladies started on their march five weeks previously, and held a meeting every evening, except Sundays, getting signatures for their petition en route. They carried a banner announcing their object and were*

accompanied by a covered van which contained the petition. The leader was Mrs. de Fonblanque. Only six of the ladies had walked the whole 386 miles from Edinburgh but others had joined en route, some coming from Durham and another from Stockton-on-Tees. They wore thick brown serge costumes, brown boots and hats with green rosettes, the leading wearing green armlets. The contingent held a meeting at Barnet on Friday night and then came on to North Finchley the assembly from the last stage of the journey being at Tally Ho! Corner. A large crowd of people turned out to watch the suffragettes but there was no demonstration of any kind." (25)

When the march reached Camden Town Tube Station, a body of supporters some 4,000 to 5,000 strong joined the procession. There were representatives from many suffrage groups including the WFL, WSPU, the 'Women's Tax Resistance League' (WTRL), the 'Actresses' Franchise League' (AFL), Free Church and Catholic Women's Societies and many men's societies which supported votes for women. Mrs. de Fonblanque led the procession followed by the other five women, including Sarah, who had walked the whole way. Behind them was the van carrying the petition and behind this the main contingent led by Mrs. Cavendish Bentinck.

A band played *'The March of the Women'* which had been composed by Ethyl Smyth, daughter of a major-general who,

Ethel Smyth, musician and suffragette, composer of *'The March of the Women'*.

against the wishes of her family, had studied music at the Leipzig Conservatory and had achieved some renown as a composer of orchestral music, choral works and operas. She had joined the suffragette movement the previous year and was, at the time, a devoted friend of Mrs. Pankhurst.

When the march reached Trafalgar Square the women were welcomed by Mrs. Despard and a meeting was held with the Square packed to capacity with supporters and onlookers. A jubilant Mrs. de Fonblanque told the crowds:

> *"The country is with us, that is the message the women marchers bring you today. We have made friends everywhere."*
> (26)

After several speeches the leaders moved on to Downing Street where Mrs. de Fonblanque, accompanied by Miss Margaret Byham, took the petition to No. 10 where it was received by the Prime Minister's secretary. Mrs. Arncliffe-Sennett was disappointed that Mr. Asquith himself did not meet the women and receive the petition believing that a statesman should not hand over his duties to a secretary.

It is sad to note that, after what was an heroic physical achievement by the six marchers, and by Sarah at the age of 62 in particular, she felt that although the march had attracted a lot of good publicity for the movement, it had achieved no positive results. She attributed later progress to the continuing militant actions:

> *". . . as far as Mr. Asquith was concerned our efforts were simply useless, as we knew they would be – when did voteless people ever win anything by peaceful means? It is pleasant to look at the silver Maltese Cross presented to the six stalwarts who did the whole march, and to note the date on it – 15th November 1912 – the day we arrived in London. The fact that during the next two years the picture galleries, palaces and places of public amusement were only open partially, if at all, and that an Act of Parliament (a last effort to make it possible*

Sir James Lowther, later Lord Ullswater, Speaker of the House of Commons 1905-1921.

to punish the intolerable suffragettes) was hurried through, was not due to our march but to the vigorous campaign of destruction which succeeded it (still, the march must have advertised the movement)". [2]

On 23rd and 24th January 1913 the *Franchise and Registration Bill,* which had received its first reading the previous June and had passed its second in July, was debated again in the House of Commons. The proposal was that amendments should be inserted which would include suffrage for women. However, the Conservative leader approached the Speaker, Sir James Lowther, and suggested that the inclusion of these amendments would change the substance of the Bill to the extent that it would have to be withdrawn and revised for reintroduction at a later date.

On 27th January Sir James announced to the Commons that, after due consideration, he had to agree that the inclusion of women would have this effect and, there being no means of appeal against a ruling by the Speaker, the Government withdrew the measure.

Needless to say, the response from the WSPU was immediate and heated. A fresh campaign of window smashing was launched and, despite the fact that Harry Gordon Selfridge had publically supported their cause, his department store in Oxford Street, which had opened four years earlier, was earmarked for attack. Sarah was selected for the deed.

"I entered the arena again in Feb. 1913. I undertook to break some windows at Selfridges. Of course I walked round and round the block of buildings beforehand. I found that all the

157

Selfridge's Store in Oxford Street – the first store in London to install women's lavatories.

RUSS LONDON

windows were the same size and all separated by flat slabs of stone and I thought that, if I could avoid notice till quite close to the stone, I might manage to break a window each side of it. I left my home about 8 p.m. on Friday 7th. February and went to friends near Portman Square and had supper. The best time was considered just before the theatres came out. I was in Seymour Street just before 11.30 and I found the streets simply alive with policemen; they were chatting at every street corner and signalling to each other and my courage failed me, or perhaps it was quite as much my intense dislike of attracting attention to myself, of being in any way prominent, which made me turn back in the direction of my friends' house; but then I decided this would never do, I had promised to break the windows and it had to be done. I had my right hand on the handle of my hammer when I turned round and walked steadily past two policemen. I knew I must do it in full view and, at lightning speed, to draw my hammer out of its hiding place and give a mighty blow which went right through the first window; and then I felt my left arm grasped by a policeman. Perhaps this weakened me, at any rate I felt now as if I were

METROPOLITAN POLICE.

D Division.

Marylebone Lane Station.

Take Notice, that you *Sarah Benett*

are bound in the sum of *Fifty* Pounds to

appear at the *Marlboro. St.* Police Court, situated at

Marlboro Street at *Ten*

o'clock *A* M., on the *8th* day of *February*

19*13*, to answer the charge of* *Wilful damage*

and unless you then appear there, further proceedings will be taken.

Dated this *8th* day of *February*

One Thousand Nine Hundred *13*

G. Webber Insp

Officer on Duty.

* Being found drunk in a public street, or being guilty, while drunk, of disorderly behaviour in a street
or whatever the charge may be.

20000 | 9 | 09. M.P. 81b

Harry Gordon Selfridge, a stalwart supporter of the suffragettes in spite of their attacks on his store.

hacking away at cheese. I immediately cracked the second window but it took two or three blows to make a hole in it. I said nothing to the two policemen who marched me to the station near except: "don't pinch my arm" who then changed his hold to the sleeve of my coat. On our arrival, I was searched by a woman full of sympathy and Selfridges manager was sent for to charge me, and stated that the broken windows were each worth £80. I was left in the custody of one policeman, who wanted to be chatty, but I would not take the trouble to talk to him. The two policemen who marched me to the station wanted to know why I attacked Selfridge, who was friendly to us. I did not answer, though that question exercised my mind later, and I insisted on seeing the important person who had sent me a request to do it but could get no explanation or sympathy from her. Several other policemen came and looked at us and one exclaimed ruefully: "how I wish she had done it last week when I was on the beat." Then the manager appeared. Then I gave my friends' phone number and she very soon came and bailed me and we went back to her house together feeling we had earned a night's rest. We were up early and at Marlborough Street police station by 10 o'clock. Here I was with a delicate, interesting girl who had also broken windows near Oxford Street the night before. She was at almost the last stage of exhaustion and, as she had the white skin which goes with reddish hair she looked, as she lay on the floor of the cell we jointly occupied, almost unearthly. She had resolved that she would refuse bail and refuse food and break windows every time she was released and she was in the exalted frame of mind which goes with the resolve to give one's life – gentle and composed and free of anger. (However, the illness of her father prevented her carrying out her plan.) She was taken back to Holloway from which she had just been released and I was bailed, after having been remanded to the Cleverness Assizes on the 20th of the month, but my case was not taken that day and I had to go again on 21st. I had domestic worries to contend with and was in a highly nervous irritable mood. Our friends were not allowed in Court and it seemed to me that there was no woman there besides myself; afterwards I learned there were one or two. My friend, Mrs. Arncliffe-Sennett, had pinned a charming 4-leaved shamrock in turquoises and pearls on my dress and perhaps that acted as a talisman, but I made my carefully-prepared speech to the jury without hesitation or mistake. Mr. Wallace was again the Judge as he had been at Newington. He was gentle and kind in his manners and I thought, as on the previous occasion, that his sympathies are with us. Two policemen were put in the witness box and repeated the absurd story they had concocted about my doings on the 7th but I did not think it worth while to say anything. The one person who was not rehearsed, to whom the whole procedure of a court is unfamiliar, is just the one to whom it is of such vital importance to do exactly the right thing – the prisoner in the dock. I suppose we have always felt that our appeal was to a larger court – the Court of Public Opinion and of the

future – we don't mean to let the verdict of twelve jurymen and a judge, whose office is just a comfortable livelihood to him, be final. Some dozen of us were tried that day and all had long sentences; mine was six months. I asked Mr. Wallace if I might see my friends before going to Holloway and he said that was a matter for the Police Commissioners, but did not tell me how they were to be got at. However, my stalwart friend, Mrs. Sennett, did not wait to see me. As soon as sentence was passed on me and I was in Holloway, . . . I at once refused food, as I had told Mr. Wallace I should, but I think I took water. I was not in good health and the fast rapidly affected me. I was kept in solitary confinement but allowed books and, during Saturday 22nd, I read steadily almost the whole of 'Shelley's Poetical Works' and they appealed to me as never before. Then on Sunday I read 'Corinne' * which I had brought with me. When I got up on Monday I did not quite faint but I felt as if I were dying. I said to myself: "this is quite right, quite what we are all prepared for" but I rang the bell and told the wardress who answered it and the Doctor came to me. Then in the afternoon three important-looking doctors came together and examined and talked to me (I had not the least objection to being released and made out as bad a case as I could) largely as a consequence, as I discovered afterwards, of the intervention of my doughty friend Mrs. Sennett. Soon after they left, the Governor (a doctor) and the prison Doctor both came to tell me that I was to be released next day and to beg me to take food, which I consented to do. The Governor felt my icy cold hands and seemed honestly pleased that he could release me. I heard one or two cries as cell doors were opened and closed again and I knew that the torture of forcible feeding, to which I have never been submitted, was beginning for my

Opposite: **A contemporary cartoon showing a robust suffragette refusing food in prison until she had lost sufficient weight to squeeze through the bars and rejoin her companions.**

younger and less fortunate comrades. It was just before the 'Cat and Mouse Bill' had become law. So on 26th February I was released unconditionally, having done four days of my six months sentence." [2]

The *Cat and Mouse Act* or more properly *The Prisoners' (Temporary Discharge for Ill-health) Act 1913* was introduced by the Government to address the growing problem of hunger striking by suffragette prisoners. The Act provided for the early release of prisoners who had been weakened by fasting to the point where they were at risk of death. When their health had recovered, they were supposed to be recalled to prison to complete their sentence though, in reality, few did.

It was known as the *Cat and Mouse Act* as it resembled the cruel action of a cat which releases its captured prey only to pounce upon it again, to torment it some more, just when it thought it was free.

* **"Corinne" a book by Madame de Staël published in 1810 about a woman isolated from mankind by her own intelligence.**

THE CAT AND MOUSE ACT
PASSED BY THE LIBERAL GOVERNMENT

THE LIBERAL CAT
ELECTORS VOTE AGAINST HIM!
KEEP THE LIBERAL OUT!

BUY AND READ 'THE SUFFRAGETTE' PRICE 1D

9. Birmingham

July 1913

In the summer of 1912, the WSPU had moved their headquarters from the property in Clements Inn owned by the Pethick-Lawrences to an impressive building on Kingsway known as Lincoln's Inn House. Later in the same year the separation of the Union from its erstwhile benefactors was completed when the Pethick-Lawrences had been expelled from the WSPU.

With the increasing violence and destruction of property being undertaken by the WSPU, the Home Office was now determined to use much stronger measures to control them. In February, after the attempt to burn down the house in Walton-on-the-Hill, Surrey which was being built for Lloyd George, Emmeline Pankhurst had publically declared:

> *"For all that has been done in the past I accept full responsibility. That I have advised, I have incited, I have conspired."*
> (27)

After such a complete and damning confession she was arrested and charged with *"Procuring or inciting women to commit offences contrary to the Malicious Injuries to Property Act"*. On 2nd April she was tried, found guilty and sentenced to three years' imprisonment. Not long after admission to Holloway she announced she was going on hunger strike and on 25th April the *Cat and Mouse Act,* after an extraordinarily swift passage through parliamentary procedures, received Royal Assent.

On 30th April 1913 the new Headquarters building on Kingsway was raided by police and a vanload of papers taken away to be examined for the names and details of financial donors who might then be threatened with prosecution for supporting an organisation engaged in illegal activities. Leading members of the headquarters staff, Flora Drummond, Harriet Kerr, Rachel Barrett, Beatrice Sanders and Agnes Lake were arrested. Landlords

The police raid on the WSPU headquarters on Kingsway on 30th April 1913. The hired removal van parked outside was filled with records which were confiscated for examination.

of public buildings were told not to let premises to suffragist bodies, meetings in public parks were banned and the printers of '*The Suffragette*', the new newspaper of the WSPU, were charged with incitement thereby forcing publication, which was never interrupted, underground. An attempt by the Government to have the telephone lines to Lincoln's Inn House cut was foiled by the General Post Office who refused to do what they considered to be an illegal act.

Despite the proscription of meetings in public parks, Sarah and many of her militant colleagues defied the ban:

167

Emily Davison lies fatally injured after attempting to intercept the King's horse, *Anmer,* in the Derby on 4th June 1913.

"It was not long before I was in harness again. The W.S.P.U. offices had been raided, the Hyde Park meetings had been prohibited but I was among those who defied the police and held meetings still. We were conducted out of the Park at the Marble Arch where mounted police held the gates. Then I became fiercely militant again. I am sure that I was suspected and often followed by police or detectives; when I came home at night from my errands (not of mercy) there seemed to be a good many police, some with bicycles, on the watch near my house; but they had no grounds for arresting me. Once, a little man got out of the Tube when I did and followed me to the Emerson Club and waited till I had dined and then followed me again; but I managed to shake him off by making believe I was going up in the lift and then dodging to the other side and going back a few stations. When I finally came to the upper air at Camden Town he was nowhere." [2]

On 4th June 1913 an event took place which was to become perhaps the most iconic action of the entire suffrage campaign. Emily Davison intercepted the King's racehorse in the Epsom Derby and died from her injuries four days later. At the time the generally held opinion was that she had thrown herself under the horse's hooves to publicise her cause through martyrdom. Today it is thought more likely that, although she realised the danger of her action, and was prepared to die if necessary, she was more probably intent upon hanging a *"Votes for Women"* banner on the horse. Either way, she became a martyr to the cause and her death received worldwide publicity.

Emily Wilding Davison was friendly with, and greatly admired by, Sarah who had taken part in operations with her and had served time alongside her in Holloway. On one occasion Sarah had arranged, at Emily's request, to smuggle a watch into her in prison. She was a fervent believer in the WSPU slogan – *"Deeds not Words"*. She had been arrested nine times and had been force-fed on 49 occasions. She was an innovator with great determination and had been the first activist to set fire to a pillar box.

Sarah felt strongly about the reaction to Emily's death from certain sections of the public and later wrote the following contemptuous note:

"I was grimly amused at a newspaper saying men had come away from the 'Derby Day' on which Emily Davison gave her life who, as they left the course, never mentioned the fact and seemed unconscious of it. Did not the writer know that there are men, (perhaps a large proportion of those who attend race meetings are such), who are like crawling reptiles, unwitting of anything which has no appeal in it to their narrow selfish interests, especially is this their attitude towards women who simply don't exist for them except so far as they minister to their comforts." [2]

Emily Davison's return ticket to London from Epsom Racecourse which supported the view that she had not intended to become a martyr.

169

The funeral procession of Emily Davison in her home town of Morpeth, Northumberland, where she was interred in her family plot.

Emily's funeral on 14th June 1913 was orchestrated by the WSPU into an event which attracted nationwide interest and publicity for the cause all over the world. The coffin was brought from Epsom to Victoria Station from where it was paraded through the streets of London to St. George's, Bloomsbury, where the funeral service was held. Some 6,000 suffragists took part in the procession dressed either in white carrying laurel wreaths, or in black carrying purple irises, or in purple with crimson peonies. Many clergymen and university graduates marched in their gowns.

Past Buckingham Palace and down Piccadilly the route was lined with tens of thousands of people who maintained a respectful silence. From King's Cross the coffin was taken by train to Emily's home town of Morpeth, in Northumberland, for interment in her family plot in the churchyard of St. Mary the Virgin. On her gravestone was carved the slogan of the WSPU, *"Deeds not Words"* an objective which, perhaps above all others, she had struggled to achieve. An annual pilgrimage to Emily's grave in Morpeth was instituted and in 1916 this was organised by Sarah Benett. Mr. Asquith and his principal ministers were still the number one targets of the suffragettes and when the WSPU headquarters learned that the Prime Minister was to speak at a meeting in Birmingham, on Monday 21st July, Sarah was asked if she would go:

" . . . *I agreed at once and on Saturday July 19th, just when our village was celebrating its annual festival, I trudged off with a small suitcase.*

"*I was upset not to be met at Birmingham Station and not to find the Office open however, when I went a second time, Miss M. was there and directed me to my hotel where I gave an assumed name. I was busy on Sunday getting familiar with Birmingham and its suburbs and, especially, of the scene of our proposed action. On Monday morning we had plenty to do deciding on the parts each of us should take, meeting at the Office whilst avoiding the notice of the police. Finally, we met at the Office for 4 o'clock tea and I made a very substantial tea with an eye to contingencies. Then the question who should open the proceedings arose and I was asked to.*

"*My little straw bag was laden with three heavy half-bricks and, with it on my arm, I started alone up the hill in the direction of the Grand Hotel where Asquith was lodging. Have you ever felt your tongue cleave to the roof of your mouth? I don't know why but I did then! I soon arrived at the side window of the hotel which I had carefully noted beforehand. There was no crowd, still the street was fairly full and I was amazed, when my first brick fell heavily on the pavement instead of breaking the window, that no one appeared to have noticed. My second brick went through the window and landed on the floor inside and then, to make sure, I threw the third brick after it through the same window. I was then a prisoner and being pushed in front of two policemen towards the Station through an excited crowd whose attention was divided as six or eight others soon joined me in custody at the Station.*

The Grand Hotel, Birmingham, c 1900.

"At Birmingham, on two occasions, I experienced more ruffianliness than anywhere except, perhaps, from the 'liberals' of East Fife. Even the police of Black Friday were not so wantonly cruel as the Birmingham police, and ruffianliness is the only way to describe the bearing of the Birmingham prison officials. When we were all safe in a room at the Police Station, the two constables still held my arms and I said angrily: "don't touch me" to which the reply was: "you've got to be touched" and they pushed me about the room. I gave my name as Mary Gray but was told that Miss H. had given me away as we passed her she said: "there's Miss Benett arrested" so I was tried as 'Mary Gray or Sarah Benett'. The efforts to bail us were unsuccessful; as we were guilty of 'wilful damage' we were to be kept in custody and were soon removed to the cells so I would not eat or drink. I was given a pillow and rug in a cell to myself but this is not

172

sufficient to enable one to sleep on a wooden plank with any degree of comfort, and we had nothing of our own with us. There were certainly fleas in the rug and policemen came into the wing, in which our cells were, frequently during the night but the Matron was very friendly and sympathetic and, after a wash in the morning, we went to the Police Court fairly fresh and fit. My case was heard after several of the others about midday.

"The B. [Birmingham] Court is quite round with the prisoners' dock raised in the centre. When I got into it I was conscious of crowds of men, apparently nothing but men, and mostly of the young hooligan and loafer class and I at once decided to address my remarks to these who, to my mind, have as big a grievance as women have. Their education has been a shameful failure and they have been forced to follow blind alley occupations, and been cuffed and starved till their manhood is almost destroyed. I turned to them and very simply said that, having suffered and starved during 24 hours, I was not fit to defend myself in a court dominated by men who were there every day and cared for anything rather than the prisoner.

"I turned to this public knowing I could win them to my side and told them that I had had to try to sleep on a plank in a prison cell, that I had had nothing to eat or drink for nearly 24 hours and no chance of preparing my defence; but everyone knew we were doing things hateful to us, because only in this way could we call the attention of the Government and the public to our claims. I was told afterwards that I had won the sympathies of the public. In his evidence against me the manager of the hotel said I had thrown the bricks into the lounge and smoke room, which was crowded at the time, but no one was hit, and I felt tremendously thankful that I had not injured anyone. No account seemed to be taken of my former sentences and I wondered if the London and Birmingham

courts were in communication with each other (this later). My
sentence was a month." (2)

Two women were fined 40 shillings each, plus the cost of the damage they
had caused, or a prison sentence of 21 days. Two others, one of which was
Sarah, were fined 40 shillings each, plus the cost of the damage, or prison
in the second division for a month. Sarah chose prison and declared that
she would go on hunger strike.

Though some sections of the public in Birmingham were sympathetic to
the suffragettes' cause, there were also reports of considerable hostility:

> *"In other parts of the city suffragettes were chased by hooting*
> *crowds who threatened them with violence. The women took*
> *advantage of any chance of escape, rushing into open shops*
> *and offices causing great groups of hostile people to collect."*
> (28)

His Majesty's Prison, Birmingham, always known locally as Winson Green
Prison, was opened in 1849. It had an impressive castellate frontage, as
shown in the photograph opposite, and the accommodation had been much
expanded during the late 19th century. By the time Sarah was admitted in
1913 the prison could hold 498 men and 121 women in cells measuring
13ft x 7ft x 9ft high and a women's hospital wing had been added in 1903.
Sarah considered it was the worst place to which she had ever been
committed.

> *"'Eliza', a doughty little suffragette, kept us all much amused*
> *with her pranks and jokes till a closed waggonette came to the*
> *door to take us all to Winson Green Gaol and then she led us*
> *in shouting and singing and smashing everything breakable.*
> *The small windows were soon gone and then we waved pocket*
> *handkerchiefs through the openings. 'Eliza' was the only one*
> *of us on remand she having broken a window valued at more*
> *than £5.*

Winson Green Prison, Birmingham.
This photograph was taken on 16th April 1936 before the execution of the notorious 'Nurse Waddingham' who had murdered two elderly women in her care. The Rolls Royce belonged to a protester, Violet van der Elst , a well-known campaigner against capital punishment.

"The next six days was the grimmest experience I have gone through; there was a ruthless, almost a malicious, determination in the officials to see how much we could bear but, at the same time, the privileges of Rule 243a were extended to us. We exercised every day and we were allowed books – a list of which was brought, but I found that practically everything worth reading was in use on the men's side of the prison. The Governor and Doctors were anxious to find out if I had been in prison before and were very affable and considerate until I had (inadvertently) told them; and then just as rude and merciless. The Governor would address me as "Benett" with some jeering remark (I wish I had called him "Green").

"We had an impression that we were being photographed. A friendly, chatty wardress would come for us, one at a time, to go out to exercise and passing a certain spot we thought we heard the click of the shutter.

"Only 'Eliza' and I continued to exercise after the second or third day and very soon we could not walk without the support of a wardress and collapsed on the grass when we met, finding some comfort in telling each other how ill we felt.

"I had been fasting since 4.30 on Monday 21st. – nothing, either solid or liquid, having passed my lips for over six days and, on the evening of Sunday 27th, someone came and told me I should be released the following day and asked me to take nourishment. I have to confess that I forgot for the moment that my release would not, as before, be unconditional. I wish I had said "no" as they would then have had to release me at once.

"For a few days I had been unable to move without vomiting or heaving and retching (I was not actually sick). My tongue was swelled and quite white except the tip which was covered with blisters. My emaciated body was so bruised and bed sore that I could hardly rest in any position. I had a body belt and was able to compress my empty stomach with it and, except for rheumatic pains near the heart, I did not suffer much and I think I was only half alive. I was not capable of very sustained thought and I consented to take food and, of course, a mug of strong bovril and then of water went far to revive me. Still, I was only just able to stand when next morning I was taken downstairs thinking a photographer might be in waiting somewhere. I had my long crepe scarf wrapped round my head. Then a thing happened which I could hardly have believed to be possible in civilised England. I was taken into the courtyard and told to get into a taxi waiting there, the front of it was entirely of glass and, as soon as I was seated, the driver got off his seat and walked away and a number of

Prisoners (Temporary Discharge for Ill-Health) Act, 1913.

NOTICE TO BE GIVEN TO PRISONER.

Sarah Bennett is this day discharged from *Birmingham* Prison in pursuance of the Secretary of State's Order of _*25th July 1913*_ subject to the following conditions :—

1. The prisoner shall return to the above-mentioned prison on the _*2nd*_ of _*August*_ 19*13*

2. The period of temporary discharge granted by this Order may, if the Secretary of State thinks fit, be extended on a representation by the prisoner that the state of *her* health renders *her* unfit to return to prison. If such representation be made, the prisoner shall submit *her* self, if so required, for medical examination by the Medical Officer of the above-mentioned Prison or other registered medical practitioner appointed by the Secretary of State.

3. The prisoner shall notify to the *Chief Constable of Birmingham and also to the* Commissioner of Police of the Metropolis the place of residence to which *she* goes on *her* discharge. The prisoner shall not change *her* residence without giving one clear day's previous notice in writing to the *Chief Constable and to the* Commissioner, specifying the residence to which *she* is going, and *she* shall not be temporarily absent from *her* residence for more than twelve hours without giving a like notice.

4. The prisoner shall abstain from any violation of the law.

If *she* fails to comply with any of the foregoing conditions, the prisoner is liable to be arrested and taken back to prison. While *she* is at large under this Order the currency of *her* sentence is suspended.

*Perg Green*
Governor.

detectives (four or five) came and stood in a row and stared at me; but I baffled them by drawing two folds of the scarf across my face. The Governor and Doctor and other officials seemed to have forgotten all sorts of things and, whilst they bustled about, I was kept sitting there in a state bordering on hysterics. At last we got away but halfway to Northfield one of the tyres burst and there was a long wait and again the two detectives who were following on bicycles came to stare at me without much success." (2)

Sarah had made herself seriously ill and returned to her house in Hampstead to lick her wounds and rest. She was 63 years of age and the lifestyle she had imposed upon herself had damaged her health. She was advised by her doctor and her friends that she had now done her bit for the cause and her role in the future, if any, must be a passive one.

But Sarah's days of violent protest had not ended.

10. "Tell the King!"

London, 10th March 1914

In 1906 an erotic nude painting of Venus by Velásquez was sold by its owner, John Morritt MP, to the National Arts Collection Fund who acquired it for the National Gallery. Since the painting had been bought by his ancestor in 1813 it had hung above the fireplace in his house in Yorkshire, Rokeby Hall, and had hence acquired the title of 'The Rokeby Venus'. Described by Morritt as his *"fine picture of Venus's backside"*, the painting had challenged the conservative perception of decency and was greatly admired by King Edward VII who had contributed £8,000 towards its purchase.

On the morning of 10th March 1914, a woman with a sketchbook in her hand entered the National Gallery and approached the painting which was

Black and white reproduction of *'The Rokeby Venus'* by Velásquez in the National Gallery.

PHOTO TAKEN BY SCOTLAND YARD DETECTIVE 1913 – IN PUBLIC DOMAIN

Mary Richardson who slashed 'The Rokeby Venus'.

exhibited on an easel in the centre of Room 17. She produced a meat cleaver which she had concealed up her sleeve and, before she could be restrained by the room attendant, had broken the glass and slashed the canvas several times. The woman was Mary Richardson, a Canadian-born suffragette who had been a member of the WSPU since 1909 and had recently been involved in several incidents for which she had been arrested and imprisoned.

For the vandalism to the picture Mary Richardson was sentenced to six months imprisonment. Her act, she explained, had been occasioned by the arrest on the previous day of Emmeline Pankhurst, whom she revered, at a rowdy meeting in St. Andrew's Hall, Glasgow. Her reasons were reported in *'The Times'* the following day:

"I have tried to destroy the picture of the most beautiful woman in mythological history as a protest against the Government for destroying Mrs. Pankhurst, who is the most beautiful character in modern history. Justice is an element of beauty as much as colour and outline on canvas Mrs.

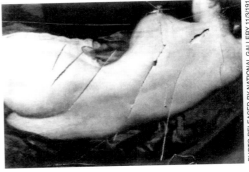

PHOTO RELEASED BY NATIONAL GALLERY 11/3/1914

Detail from black and white reproduction of 'The Rokeby Venus' showing the slashes made by Mary Richardson.

Pankhurst seeks to procure justice for womanhood, and for this she is being slowly murdered by a Government of Iscariot politicians. If there is an outcry against my deed, let every one remember that such an outcry is an hypocrisy so long as they allow the destruction of Mrs. Pankhurst and other beautiful living women, and that until the public cease to countenance human destruction the stones cast against me for the destruction of this picture are each an evidence against them of artistic as well as moral and political humbug and hypocrisy." (29)

Years later she admitted that, on a less etherial plane, she *"didn't like the way men visitors to the gallery gaped at it all day"* and later on in her career, Richardson was to join and hold high office in Sir Oswald Mosley's Blackshirt Fascist party.

There had been vandalism of paintings in the previous year when Lillian Forrester and Evelyn Manesta smashed the glass of thirteen paintings in the Manchester Art Gallery damaging some of the canvases; but Mary Richardson's audacious act in Central London gave rise to an immediate spate of copycat incidents.

On 4th May 1914, the opening day of the Royal Academy's Summer Exhibition, Mary Wood, described by *'The Times'* as an *"elderly woman of distinctly peaceable appearance"* entered the building and attacked John Singer Sarjent's portrait of Henry James. The gallery was crowded and several visitors rushed to restrain her until she was taken into custody by the police. Feelings were running high and one man, who appeared to be sympathetic and protective of the attacker, was driven out of the building having been roughed up by the crowd and his spectacles smashed. In a subsequent letter to the WSPU Mary Wood explained her actions:

"I have tried to destroy a valuable picture because I wish to show the public that they have no security for their property nor their art treasures until women are given political freedom." (30)

Grace Marcon (*aka* Frieda Graham) one of several suffragettes imprisoned for slashing paintings in 1914.

EASTERN DAILY PRESS

Eight days later Gertrude Mary Ansell attacked a portrait of the Duke of Wellington by Sir Hubert von Herkorner and on 26th May Maude Kate Smith (*aka* Mary Spencer) slashed Sir George Clausen's 'Primavera' another provocative nude. Grace Marcon (*aka* Frieda Graham) slashed five paintings and so it went on; between March and July fourteen more paintings had been attacked and nine women arrested for it.

This new form of militancy caused considerable concern among members of the general public. From the perpetrators' point of view the actions were justified as they received widespread publicity but from press and public they received almost universal outrage and condemnation. Even members of the public with no knowledge of, or interest in, art could not approve of the destruction of valuable national treasures.

Sarah Benett did not take part in the picture slashing campaign; her ill treatment in Winson Green Prison had seriously damaged her health and she had been advised by her doctor not to engage in any activities, or attend any meetings which might result in a further arrest and prison sentence. However, at the beginning of May 1914 she learned of plans being laid by Mrs. Pankhurst for a very major action later in the month from which Sarah was determined not to be excluded.

This action was inspired by an event which had taken place in Ireland in March. Irish Home Rule was due to be implemented later in the year and there were fears that the Ulster Volunteers, a body of protestants determined to remain a part of Britain, would rise up in arms against it. British troops in the Curragh, the British Army's Headquarters in Ireland, were therefore forewarned that they would be required to intervene in such an event.

Brigadier-General Hubert Gough, GOC 3rd Cavalry Brigade at the Curragh.

However, several officers, particularly those with Irish blood, were not prepared to act against their own countrymen and informed the War Office that they would resign rather than do so. The most prominent of these was Brigadier-General Hubert Gough, General Officer Commanding the 3rd Cavalry Brigade at the Curragh. Gough was dismissed and subsequently reinstated, largely due to support from General French, the Chief of the Imperial General Staff (and, incidentally, brother of the prominent suffragist Charlotte Despard), who had directly lobbied the King on behalf of the 'mutineers'. The King convened an Irish Conference at Buckingham Palace and the whole matter was eventually glossed over and explained by the War Office as a 'misunderstanding' and the British Army was never to be ordered to act against the Ulstermen.

It did not escape Mrs. Pankhurst that success in this very delicate matter had been achieved through bypassing the Government and appealing directly to the King. After years of battling against an obdurate political system, with every means known to her, and achieving nothing, a direct petition to the King seemed like the last route left open to her.

The WSPU decided to give this event maximum advance publicity as they wished large numbers of the public to attend. However, it also had the effect of attracting crowds of the wrong sort of people.

Large numbers of hostile youths gathered outside the Palace, looking for an

King George V whose intervention in the suffrage battle Mrs. Pankhurst hoped to gain.

amusing day out and a chance to goad and jostle the women. The advance warning also gave the police a chance to organise themselves in detail. The Palace grounds were searched thoroughly and guards doubled on all gates and approaches. One thousand extra policemen were drafted into the area for what promised to be an incident of special magnitude and importance. In the event, it was also a day of special significance as, unbeknown to either of them at the time, this was to be the WSPU's and Sarah Benett's last violent protest.

Accounts of the demonstration and the routes taken vary widely. Most newspapers reported that Mrs. Pankhurst, with between 100 and 200 WSPU supporters, started from Grosvenor Gardens, at the Victoria end of Grosvenor Place, where she was believed to have spent the previous night, and marched to the Wellington Arch at Hyde Park Corner where she managed to slip through the police cordon with a few other women on to Constitution Hill. The rest of her supporters were contained at the Arch by the police with whom they fought a long and bitter battle.

Other accounts say that the main assembly point was Grosvenor Square, over a mile to the north of Grosvenor Gardens, and that the march proceeded down Park Lane where Mrs. Pankhurst and a few supporters split off from the main body and cut through Mayfair and Green Park to outflank the police cordons on Constitution Hill *(see map)*.

Whichever account is correct, it is probable that Sarah Benett, calling

herself Susan Burnton at the time, was in the group which was contained by the police outside the Wellington Arch gates. She was one of the first arrests made and was one of those who were detained after the demonstration and sent to Holloway with Mrs. Pankhurst.

Sylvia Pankhurst was an extreme socialist who was politically much further to the left than her mother and sister. She was an active member of the 'Independent

The Wellington Arch at Hyde Park Corner.

CARLOTTA BENINI

184

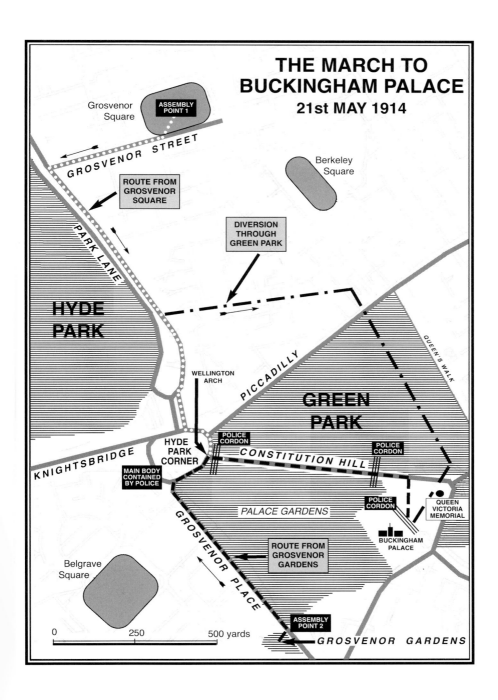

THE MARCH TO
BUCKINGHAM PALACE
21st MAY 1914

Grosvenor Square

ASSEMBLY POINT 1

GROSVENOR STREET

Berkeley Square

ROUTE FROM GROSVENOR SQUARE

DIVERSION THROUGH GREEN PARK

PARK LANE

HYDE PARK

QUEEN'S WALK

WELLINGTON ARCH

PICCADILLY

GREEN PARK

POLICE CORDON

HYDE PARK CORNER

POLICE CORDON

KNIGHTSBRIDGE

CONSTITUTION HILL

MAIN BODY CONTAINED BY POLICE

PALACE GARDENS

POLICE CORDON

QUEEN VICTORIA MEMORIAL

BUCKINGHAM PALACE

GROSVENOR PLACE

Belgrave Square

ROUTE FROM GROSVENOR GARDENS

0   250   500 yards

ASSEMBLY POINT 2

GROSVENOR GARDENS

Labour Party' whereas the WSPU rejected alliance with all political parties. There had consequently been serious family disagreements over several issues in recent months. Matters had come to a head in 1913 with Sylvia's support for the strikers in the Dublin Lock-Out, a long and bitter industrial dispute between Irish workers and employers. She was expelled from the WSPU together with the 'East London Federation of the WSPU' which she had formed and headed. She therefore changed the name to the 'East London Federation of Suffragettes' (ELFS) which, unlike the WSPU, admitted men to membership and was run democratically.

In the Buckingham Palace march Sylvia led her own contingent of the ELFS and, in the following week's edition of the ELFS newspaper '*The Woman's Dreadnought*', which she edited, she printed an account by one of her members, Daisy Parsons, who had been an eyewitness to events at the Palace. When she reached the Victoria Memorial Mrs. Parsons found a great crowd of people, mainly youths, standing with their backs to the Memorial facing the Palace.

> *"There was a wide vacant space between the people and the palace, and [in] the middle of this space was a line of police, not standing shoulder to shoulder but with a space of some yards between each one . . . Every now and then a woman would dart out from amongst the dense throng of spectators into the space, and the police rushed at her, caught her, and threw her back into the crowd. Then the young men in the crowd would turn on the woman and beat her and tear her clothes and drag down her hair and shout that she ought to be burnt. Then the woman would run out again towards the police only to be caught and thrown back again by the police and again beaten by the men. This would be repeated until at last she was hustled away out of sight or placed under arrest."* [31]

Mrs. Parsons related how she saw one woman face this eleven times before being arrested and stated that the police never attempted to protect any of the women who were assaulted.

NORAH SMYTH

Daisy Parsons (*extreme right*) **with other ELFS members** (*from left*): **Mrs. Watkins, Mrs. Jessie Payne, Miss Savoy** (*aka* **Hughes), Mrs. Bird and Mrs. Julia Scurr, presenting a petition at 10 Downing Street in July 1914.**

> "*At last the mounted police came up at a gallop and drove everyone away . . . I saw a young woman dressed in pink with a jeering crowd behind her. The young woman stopped and stood with her back against the wall. A sentry walked up to her and pushed her. She said 'How dare you', and he struck her in the face with his fist.*" (31)

Rosa May Billinghurst, a member of the WSPU, had been paralysed since childhood but took a full part in demonstrations and militant action in her hand-propelled invalid carriage which she would drive at police barriers like a battering ram. She took full advantage of her disability and consequently received little sympathy from the police who had handled her very roughly on more than one occasion.

Another ELFS member, Charlotte Drake, was with Rosa May Billinghurst outside the Palace on 22nd May and witnessed her driving her invalid carriage at the police line at full speed in her usual reckless manner.

"I was beside her. They threw us back, but we returned. Two policemen picked up the tricycle with Miss Billinghurst in it, turned it over, and dropped her on the ground. The excitement gave me strength – I picked her up bodily and lifted her back. We straightened the machine as best we could, rested a little to take breath and struggled on again. The police would not take us – only knock us about. Then in the enormous crowd I got sent flying one way and, she another. I tried to find her. It seemed as though the earth had swallowed her . . ." [32]

She was later found, according to the next day's edition of the *'Newcastle Journal'*, some distance from Hyde Park Corner. She had been severely maltreated by the crowd and was crying bitterly and in a half fainting condition. The police escorted her from the scene but made no attempt to arrest her.

Mrs. Pankhurst being arrested outside Buckingham Palace 22nd May 1914

PHOTOGRAPHER UNKNOWN – IN PUBLIC DOMAIN

Rebel with a Cause

One of the two principal battlegrounds of the day was at the Wellington Arch after the police had closed the gates to Constitution Hill and the protesters found themselves surrounded by a huge ring of mounted and foot police. Fierce fighting broke out between the frustrated suffragettes and the police with several women armed with batons and eggs which had been blown and filled with red or yellow paint. Eventually the police retaliated and organised a baton charge against the rioting women during which several of the protesters were injured and carried away in ambulances. Others, including Sarah, were arrested and taken to the small Hyde Park Corner Police Station which was located actually within the Arch. Before long there was not a window in the station which had not been smashed by the protesters.

Groups of hostile youths were gathered at the Wellington Arch as they were outside the Palace and took every opportunity to 'assist' the police in controlling and arresting the most violent of the demonstrators. Several policemen were bitten by women they were attempting to control or arrest and one policeman, Constable Tyson, was knocked unconscious by a suffragette's baton and was removed to hospital in an ambulance.

Meanwhile, Mrs. Pankhurst, whether by slipping through the gates at the Wellington Arch or by cutting through Green Park to outflank the cordons, had arrived at the Victoria Memorial outside Buckingham Palace. According to the '*Daily Telegraph*' she had been recognised by the police long before she reached the Palace:

> "*Plain clothes officers from Scotland Yard, who have been waiting to arrest her under the "Cat and Mouse" Act, had recognised her some 150 yards up Constitution Hill. At a point where the line of railings gives a view of what is known as Equerries' Entrance they impeded the militant leader's further advance. Mrs. Pankhurst was able to offer little or no resistance . . .*" [33]

The WSPU leader detached herself from the crowd and made a rush at the Palace gates but she was not recognised by the police and was pushed back into the line of protesters. She tried again and this time she was recognised by Chief Inspector Francis Harry Rolfe of 'A' Division who arrested her and carried her bodily to a waiting taxi to be transported to Canon Row Police Station and thence to Holloway. This arrest provided another of the most iconic photographs of the suffrage campaign – Mrs. Emmeline Pankhurst being carried by Chief Inspector Rolfe, her small size three-and-a-half feet clear of the ground, eyes closed in frustration and her hands clenched in protest.

Ever aware of any opportunity for publicity, she shouted out to reporters as she was carried away: *"Arrested at the gates of the Palace! Tell the King!"*

Chief Inspector Rolfe, the son of a policeman, has gained immortality through this single event but two months later tripped over a barrier when on duty and died later in St. Thomas's Hospital aged 45.

With Mrs. Pankhurst's arrest, her followers outside the Palace erupted with anger. The number of arrests made, again, varies from source to source; the *'Daily Telegraph'* stated there were fifty-six and listed twelve of the most prominent, including *"Susan Burnton of Lyme Regis"* which was, of course, Sarah's alias.

The extensive pre-publicity for the demonstration, which the WSPU had encouraged, served the suffragettes badly. It attracted large crowds of rowdy youths who had no scruples about bullying women and were encouraged by the police to manhandle the protesters and paw them sexually without fear of redress. There were no longer crowds of sympathetic citizens to offer them support; the recent destructive actions of WSPU members had lost the movement many of the friends it previously had and the crowds on this day were universally hostile. Anyone in the crowd who showed support for the women received the same brutal treatment as them from the hooligans whose behaviour was so violent and offensive that, towards the end of the day, the police were no longer engaged in controlling the women but in protecting them from the mob.

Sarah's release document dated 26th May 1914 under the *Cat and Mouse Act* which stated she must return to prison seven days later on 2nd June.

Prisoners (Temporary Discharge for Ill-Health)

Act, 1913.

NOTICE TO BE GIVEN TO PRISONER.

Susan Burnton otherwise known as Sarah Benett is this day discharged from *Holloway* Prison in pursuance of the Secretary of State's Order of *the 26th May 1914* subject to the following conditions :—

1. The prisoner shall return to the above-mentioned prison on the *second* of *June* 19*14*.

2. The period of temporary discharge granted by this Order may, if the Secretary of State thinks fit, be extended on a representation by the prisoner that the state of *her* health renders *her* unfit to return to prison. If such representation be made, the prisoner shall submit *her* self, if so required, for medical examination by the Medical Officer of the above-mentioned Prison or other registered medical practitioner appointed by the Secretary of State.

3. The prisoner shall notify to the Commissioner of Police of the Metropolis the place of residence to which *she* goes on *her* discharge. The prisoner shall not change *her* residence without giving one clear day's previous notice in writing to the Commissioner, specifying the residence to which *she* is going, and *she* shall not be temporarily absent from *her* residence for more than twelve hours without giving a like notice.

4. The prisoner shall abstain from any violation of the law.

If *she* fails to comply with any of the foregoing conditions, the prisoner is liable to be arrested and taken back to prison. While *she* is at large under this Order the currency of *her* sentence is suspended.

_____
Governor.

Prisoners (Temporary Discharge for Ill-Health) Act, 1913.

NOTICE TO BE GIVEN TO PRISONER.

Sarah Bennett otherwise Known as Susan Burton is this day discharged from *Holloway* Prison in pursuance of the Secretary of State's Order of *the 20th June 1914* subject to the following conditions :—

    1. The prisoner shall return to the above-mentioned prison on the *29th* of *June* 19*14*

    2. The period of temporary discharge granted by this Order may, if the Secretary of State thinks fit, be extended on a representation by the prisoner that the state of *her* health renders *her* unfit to return to prison. If such representation be made, the prisoner shall submit *her* self, if so required, for medical examination by the Medical Officer of the above-mentioned Prison or other registered medical practitioner appointed by the Secretary of State.

    3. The prisoner shall notify to the Commissioner of Police of the Metropolis the place of residence to which *she* goes on *her* discharge. The prisoner shall not change *her* residence without giving one clear day's previous notice in writing to the Commissioner, specifying the residence to which *she* is going, and *she* shall not be temporarily absent from *her* residence for more than twelve hours without giving a like notice.

    4. The prisoner shall abstain from any violation of the law.

    If *she* fails to comply with any of the foregoing conditions, the prisoner is liable to be arrested and taken back to prison. While *she* is at large under this Order the currency of *her* sentence is suspended.

[signature]
Governor.

The police, also, had made good use of the advance warning and were better prepared than ever before. A total of around 2,000 police were deployed on the day to control no more than a few hundred women. As the '*Daily Telegraph*' reported:

> "*There never was the slightest hope or possibility of the militants getting near the Palace. Acting within the authority of a well-known Act of Parliament, which renders processions prohibitable within a mile of Parliament – this radius includes Buckingham Palace – the police set themselves to prevent anything like a formal procession to the Royal residence. Never before in the exciting period that covers the various militant demonstrations have Scotland Yard's arrangements been made on so thorough and so elaborate a scale.*" [33]

The same evening another demonstration by suffragettes took place in Whitehall where several windows were smashed and, according to some sources, Sylvia Pankhurst was arrested (others say she was arrested outside Buckingham Palace in the afternoon). Earlier in the day police had raided a house in West London which was suspected, and proved to be, an arsenal for the militant suffragettes. Four women were arrested and a stock of hammers and bags containing flint stones were taken away by police. It was clear that they were intended for another window smashing campaign in protest against Mrs. Pankhurst's arrest.

Having been sentenced at Bow Street on Friday 22nd May, Sarah was taken to Holloway where she immediately went on hunger strike. Four days later, on Tuesday 26th, in view of her age and frail condition, she was released under the *Cat and Mouse Act* with orders to return to the prison one week later on 2nd June.

This she ignored and remained at liberty for a further two weeks being rearrested on Tuesday 16th. Again she announced that she did not intend to eat and four days later, on Saturday 20th, was once more released under the *Cat and Mouse Act* with orders to return nine days later on Monday 29th.

Sarah's release document dated 20th June 1914 under the *Cat and Mouse Act* **which was issued following her rearrest for failing to return under the terms of her previous release.**

This was Sarah's last term of imprisonment. She failed to return to Holloway on 29th and there is no record of any attempt to rearrest her. It is probable that the authorities had had enough of her and decided to leave her alone.

The destructive militancy of the WSPU members, their hunger strikes and the perceived futility of the *Cat and Mouse Act* were generating increasing resentment among the public. The following letter to the Editor of the '*Hull Daily Mail*' on 25th May 1914, reflected the opinion of many:

> *"Sir, — The latest exploits of the Militant Suffragettes [in] London again brings us before the necessity for a different procedure [on] the part of the Government. Certainly, things are coming to a pretty pass. These creatures wish to be placed on an equality with men. Well, why not satisfy them, and begin by treating Suffragettes [in] prison in exactly the same way as male criminals would [be] treated. The present method is a mere farce, and only succeeds in making a laughing-stock of the law. To sentence a woman to three months or six months, [as] the case may be, and let her out after four or five days because she refuses food, is absolutely ridiculous. [We] have a man in Hull now — the great Sacco —who professes to abstain from all food for 50 days at a time. Unless he is a fraud it seems to me these women are not really in any danger after a four or five days' fast. And even if they are, it is of their own seeking, and they should [be] made to stand the consequences. Certainly they should not be in a position [to] insult members of the Royal Family and assault Cabinet Ministers [at] will, and simply laugh at the law afterwards. If there is no other way, why not take it out of them financially? Any damage they may [do] to works of art, buildings, etc., make them pay for it to the utmost farthing. Leave no possession of these fanatics sacred, even to the beds they lie upon, [get] satisfaction for damage done by them. Less of money and personal effects may help to bring them to a rational state of mind when other*

things fail. I sincerely trust [we] shall be able to give a Royal welcome to our King and Queen next month without interference from these pests.

I am, Sir, etc., " WEARY." May 1914" [34]

However, world events were shortly to eclipse the struggle for women's suffrage. On Sunday 28th June, the day before Sarah was supposed to return to Holloway, the Archduke Franz Ferdinand of Austria, heir to the throne of Austria-Hungary, was assassinated in Sarajevo by Gavrilo Princip a Yugoslav nationalist.

On 3rd August, after a month of diplomatic turmoil, Germany declared war on France and the next day on Belgium. In response to this, at 7 pm on Tuesday 4th August, Britain declared war on Germany and the First World War was under way.

11. War!

4th August 1914

Mrs. Pankhurst received the news of Britain's declaration of war on Germany when she was recovering, at St. Malo in Brittany, from her most recent term in prison. She immediately decreed that militant activity by WSPU members should cease immediately for the duration of the conflict. Sarah was effectively grounded.

Two months earlier on 11th June 1914, three weeks after the March to Buckingham Palace, an exchange in the House of Commons had illustrated the division of opinion on the Government's handling of suffragette militancy and the growing realisation that the women's demands could not be swept under the political carpet indefinitely.

Lord Robert Gascoyne-Cecil a Conservative Member of Parliament and a son of Lord Salisbury, three times Prime Minister, suggested that the only people who were satisfied with the way the militancy was being handled were the Government themselves. He stated that the problem would never be satisfactorily addressed until all Members of the House understood the sense of injustice and depth of feeling felt by the protesters and their fanatical loyalty to, and trust in, their leaders. He condemned the Police brutality on Black Friday and the barbaric practice of force-feeding in prison and denounced the duplicity of the authorities with their graded treatment of prisoners according to social position as had been demonstrated by Lady Constance Lytton (*aka* mill girl 'Jane Warton').

Lord Robert Gascoyne-Cecil, Conservative MP and a son of Lord Salisbury the former Prime Minister.

HARRIS & EWING COLLECTION, LIBRARY OF CONGRESS

LESLIE WARD, VANITY FAIR 31 OCTOBER 1906

Rt. Hon. Reginald McKenna, Home Secretary 1911-1915.
(Black and White reproduction of the "Spy" caricature)

But despite his sympathy for the suffragettes, Lord Robert still strongly disapproved of their militancy and advocated deportation for convicted offenders.

Reginald McKenna, the Home Secretary, replied that the Government should not be blamed for its record so far in countering a situation absolutely without precedent in the country's history. Part of the problem, he explained, was the level of support which the suffragettes received from well-to-do, upper- and middle-class people:

"The number of women who commit crimes of that kind is extremely small, but the number of those who sympathise with them is extremely large. One of the difficulties which the police have in detecting this form of crime in bringing home the offence to the criminal is that the criminals find so many sympathisers among the well-to-do and thoroughly respectable classes that the ordinary administration of the law is rendered comparatively impossible." [35]

Mr. McKenna stated that he was inundated with suggestions from the public on how the hunger-striking suffragettes should be dealt with. These fell broadly into four groups: the first was to let them die which, he said, was overwhelmingly the most frequently offered solution and, in his opinion, would not only outrage the general public but would swell the ranks of potential martyrs; secondly was the course suggested by Lord Robert Cecil – to deport them, which McKenna considered would only shift the problem to another location; thirdly to class them as lunatics which was fraught with difficulties and offered no real solution to the problem and no deterrent to others; suffragettes regarded such brandings as badges of honour. The final solution, of course, would be to yield to the women's demands and give them the vote.

The Home Secretary believed that the best way of dealing with the problem would be to identify and cut off the women's source of funding:

> *" The militants live only by the subscriptions of rich women who themselves enjoy all the advantages of wealth secured for them by the labour of others and use their wealth against the interests of society, paying their unfortunate victims to undergo all the horrors of a hunger and thirst strike in the commission of a crime. Whatever feelings we may have against the wretched women who for 30 shillings and £2 a week go about the country burning and destroying, what must our feelings be for the women who give their money to induce the perpetration of these crimes and leave their sisters to undergo the punishment while they live in luxury. If we can succeed against them we will spare no pains. If the action is successful in the total destruction of the means of revenue of the Women's Social and Political Union I think we shall see the last of the power of Mrs. Pankhurst and her friends."* [35]

Mr. Keir Hardie, founder and leader of the Labour Party which supported universal suffrage, and a close friend of Sylvia Pankhurst, who shared his aspirations, expressed his regret that the House was discussing means of punishing the militant women instead of addressing the cause of their disaffection:

> *"We may not today discuss the question of the franchise, but surely it was possible for the Home Secretary, without any transgression of the rules of the House, to have held out just a ray of hope for the future as to the intentions of the Govern-*

JOHN FURLEY LEWIS

James Keir Hardie Founder of the Labour Party and the first ever Labour Member of Parliament.

NATIONAL PORTRAIT GALLERY NPGX35527

Josiah Clement Wedgwood, 1st Baron Wedgwood, a strong advocate of women's suffrage.

ment in regard to this most urgent question. On that point, may I say that I am not one of those who believe that a right thing should be withheld because some of the advocates of it resort to weapons of which we do not approve. That note has been sounded more than once, and if it be true, and it is true, that a section of the public outside are strongly opposed to this conduct, it is equally true that the bulk of the people look with a very calm and indifferent eye upon what is happening so long as the vote is withheld from women." (35)

The debate was joined by Josiah Clement Wedgwood, MP for Newcastle-upon-Lyme and a Staffordshire County Councillor. He was a great-great-grandson of the famous potter, Josiah Wedgwood, and would have been well known to Sarah due to his involvement in the affairs of the Potteries. He was also a strong supporter of the Suffragists. He told the House:

"We are dealing with a problem which is a very serious one indeed. To my mind, when you find a large body of public opinions, and a large number of people capable of going to these lengths, there is only one thing for a respectable House of Commons to do, and that is to consider very closely and clearly whether the complaints of those who complain are or are not justified. We are not justified in acting in panic. What it is our duty to do is to consider the rights and wrongs of these people who have acted in this way. I attribute myself no value to the vote, but I do think that when we seriously consider the

question of Woman Suffrage, which has not been done by this House up to the present, we should remember that when you see people capable of this amount of self-sacrifice, that the one duty of the House of Commons is not to stamp the iron heel upon them, but to see how far their cause is just, and to act according to justice." [(35)]

Wedgwood later had a distinguished military and political career and was ennobled in 1942 a year before his death.

Immediately after Britain's entry into the war the Government proposed the release of all suffragettes in prison on condition that they undertook not to engage in militant acts again. This was firmly refused and four days later they were released unconditionally.

The objectives of the WSPU remained unchanged and members were urged to continue the fight for suffrage although militant tactics were to be abandoned. Remembering the earlier words of their leader: *"War is not the women's way! To the women of this Union human life is sacred"* members were inclined to look upon the war with disapproval. However, as matters became more clear, the various suffrage organisations started to split into two groups – one condemning the war and advocating pacifism and the other giving support to the nation's war plans and armed services.

The WSPU came out firmly on the side of support but Sylvia Pankhurst widened the rift with her mother and sister Christabel by ardently aligning herself with the women's groups advocating pacifism. Her other sister, Adela, was active in the Women's Party of Australia which supported the pacifist cause. Mrs.

Adela Pankhurst Walsh, the least-known of the three Pankhurst daughters, who promoted suffrage for women and pacifism in Australia.

Chrystal MacMillan, delegate at the Hague Congress and a founder of the 'Women's International League for Peace and Freedom'.

Emily Hobhouse, originator of the Open Christmas Letter and a British delegate at the Women's Peace Congress at The Hague in 1915.

Pankhurst publicly condemned Sylvia and Adela saying in a letter to Sylvia: *"I am ashamed to know where you and Adela stand."*

In December 1914 Emily Hobhouse, who had already gained fame through her exposure of the concentration camps for Boer prisoners in the South African War, and subsequently for the welfare of their inmates and their dependants, wrote an 'Open Christmas Letter' to the women of Germany and Austria. This letter urged women of the world to unite in the cause of peace and was signed by over 100 British suffragists including Sylvia Pankhurst. It was well received and published in Germany and helped to confirm the solidarity between women's suffrage groups in Europe in spite of the war. On 1st March 1915 a reply signed by over 100 German suffragists was sent by Rosa Meyreder and was published in the *'Jus Suffragii'* the Journal of the International Woman Suffrage Alliance. The letter began:

HTTP://DE.WIKIPEDIA.ORG/WIKI/BILD:ROSAMEYREDERHNHNEUNZAUNDERTFUENF.JPG

Rosa Meyreder a prominent German suffragist who pledged solidarity with her British sisters.

"To our English sisters, sisters of the same race, we express in the name of many German women our warm and heartfelt thanks for their Christmas greetings, which we only heard of lately. This message was a confirmation of what we foresaw—that women of the belligerent countries, with all faithfulness, devotion, and love to their country, can go beyond it and maintain true solidarity with the women of other belligerent nations, and that really civilised women never lose their humanity . . ." [36]

Next, early in 1915, an initiative emanating from a Dutch women's suffrage group, called for a 'Women's Peace Congress' to be held in The Hague, the main purpose of which was to urge world leaders towards a truce between belligerent nations during which peace terms could be negotiated. It also proposed that quarrels between nations should be settled by arbitration, that no territory should be ceded to another nation without the consent of its inhabitants and, of course, the expected demand for women's suffrage and for women to be involved in government.

Women's groups in Britain were split with leading figures in the suffrage movement coming out on different sides. Sylvia Pankhurst, Emily Hobhouse and Emmeline Pethick-Lawrence were in favour of it, Emmeline and Christabel Pankhurst were violently opposed to it. The plea carried in the 16th April edition of *'The Suffragette'* stated:

Lida Gustava Heymann, leading German feminist and suffragist who was one of Germany's delegates at The Hague Congress.

"It is a thousand times more the duty of the militant suffragettes to fight the Kaiser for the sake of liberty than it was to fight anti-suffrage governments." [37]

The Congress went ahead with more than 1,200 delegates from 12 countries. Germany sent 28 including Lida Gustava Heymann, a huge figure among German feminists and fighters for women's suffrage. Only three of the proposed 120 strong British delegation made it, Emmeline Pethick-Lawrence, Chrystal MacMillan and Emily Hobhouse, as the Government had forbidden operation of the Folkestone-Flushing ferry for non-military traffic during the event. The French government had banned its delegates from attending altogether. The delegation from the United States included Jane Addams and Emily Balch, both future recipients of the Nobel Peace Prize.

The Congress opened on 28th April with an address by Dr. Aletta Jacobs the Dutch instigator of the event:

"With mourning hearts we stand united here. We grieve for many brave young men who have lost their lives

Aletta Jacobs, instigator of 'The Hague Congress', who was the first woman to graduate from a Dutch university and the first female doctor in Holland.

on the battlefield before attaining their full manhood; we mourn with the poor mothers bereft of their sons; with the thousands of young widows and fatherless children, and we feel that we can no longer endure in this twentieth century of civilization that government should tolerate brute force as the only solution of international disputes." [38]

The Congress resulted in the establishment of the 'International Committee of Women for Permanent Peace' (ICWPP) which was later renamed the 'Women's International League for Peace and Freedom' (WILPF) with headquarters in Geneva. The organisation still exists today though its aims may have strayed somewhat from its original aspirations; it is difficult to equate opposition to homophobia and racism with the quest for world peace.

With militant activity suspended, the most active members of the women's groups turned their considerable energy towards welfare among the poor and uneducated, particularly those families and dependants affected by the war. In London's East End Sylvia's ELFS fought against the profiteering which inevitably emerges in war conditions and provided advice and support for those suffering from loss of employment or slow payment of pensions and allowances. They set up mother and baby clinics, day nurseries and centres providing advice to families whose men were at the front.

Mrs. Pankhurst attempted to establish an organisation for the care of illegitimate children but she found that the ease of recruiting the financial support which she had enjoyed before the war was no longer there. It was not a project which was attractive to straight-laced middle class ladies who had no wish to be associated with the results of immoral liaisons and, besides, with a war on, there were far more important causes to concern them. To ease her disappointment, Mrs. Pankhurst adopted four babies herself in the hope that this would mobilise some enthusiasm and support but nothing was forthcoming.

MARGARET SARGANT FLORENCE WTRL

Emblem of the Women's Tax Resistance League.

205

War!

Clemence Housman, who was imprisoned in 1911 for non-payment of taxes, at a meeting of the 'Women's Tax Resistance League'.

Sarah, deprived of opportunities for militant demonstrations, exercised her still burning sense of injustice by involvement with the 'Women's Tax Resistance League'. The League had been founded in 1909 with the purpose of withholding taxes in protest against the exclusion of women from the vote. One of its earliest members was popular novelist Beatrice Harraden who was also a member of the WSPU and the 'Women Writers' Suffrage League'. She summarised the importance of the WTRL's work in 1913:

> *"The least any woman can do is to refuse to pay taxes, especially the tax on actually earned income. This is certainly the most logical phase of the fight for suffrage. It is a culmination of the Government's injustice and stupidity to ask*

> *that we pay an income tax on income earned by brains, when they are refusing to consider us eligible to vote."* [39]

Harraden had studied in London and Dresden, had travelled extensively in Europe and had a Bachelor of

Beatrice Harraden, writer and WSPU member who advocated non-payment of taxes.

Arts degree, another sad example of the absurdity and injustice of clever and well educated women being denied the vote.

In 1913 Mrs. Maud Arncliffe-Sennett had founded the 'Northern Men's Federation for Women's Suffrage' and in 1916 Sarah Benett, despite the fact that the WSPU excluded men from its ranks, sent her a donation to enable her to appoint a former WSPU member as organiser of the Federation. Sarah must have harboured a fellow feeling for the men, whose number included many who were prominent in local government, and been impressed by their resolve as one of their first actions was to emulate the women's march from Scotland to London the previous year in which Sarah had played a prominent part.

Mrs. Arncliffe-Sennett who had crossed swords with Sarah on several occasions when they worked together on the committee of the WFL, received widespread support for the new Federation. Many men had, in fact, been ardent supporters of 'Votes for Women' from the earliest days of the campaign but this new initiative, harnessing the enthusiasm of a growing number of influential men from north of the border, received valuable publicity for the cause.

George Lansbury, for whose election Sarah had canvassed in the Bow by-election in 1912, wrote to Mrs. Arncliffe-Sennett:

"When the history of our time is written, Mr. Asquith and his Government will be held up to the execration of all right thinking men and women, as the Prime Minister and Government which introduced and persisted in the very worst measures of torture and degradation against women fighting on behalf of truth and justice. I am no longer a Liberal in the ordinary sense, but I come from that stalwart band of radicals, who in Scotland lived and died for the Covenant, and who in Wales held on high the flag of civil and religious liberty; and today it is the men who **masquerade** *as Liberals who are false to all the traditions of political freedom their ancestors fought for. But we shall win out. The cause we represent, the freedom of the race must, and will, win."* [40]

Israel Zangwill put all his hopes in the North from where, he believed, the immediate pressure for women's suffrage to be placed on the Government's next programme must come:

> *"The formation of the Northern Men's Federation is the only gleam of hope that has lately appeared on the suffragist horizon. And unless we work hard, even the next General Election will be run on Home Rule or the Land Question, with Suffrage side-tracked. Steps must immediately be taken to get one or other of the parties to place it on its programme. I put all my hopes on the North. Even in Europe it is the Northern countries that have the Suffrage. Had the North risen earlier, Women's Suffrage would not have become a burning question."* [40]

Mary Leigh (*née* Brown) was a Manchester school teacher who joined the WSPU in 1906 and soon became a fervent activist. In 1908 she was appointed Drum Major of the 'WSPU Fife & Drum Band' which appeared regularly at marches and gatherings. Of athletic build, she took a full part in the Union's most violent activities – throwing stones at politicians, breaking windows and destroying property. In 1908 when Mr. Asquith was addressing a meeting in the Bingley Hall, Birmingham, from which women had been excluded, she and another woman climbed onto the roof of the adjacent house which they proceeded to destroy with axes, throwing down the slates onto the police below and onto the roof of the hall where the noise disrupted the meeting. The women ignored the demands of the police and angry stewards to come down and continued their destructive work as the police stoned them and trained fire hoses on them. Eventually, three policemen had to climb onto the roof and drag them down forcibly.

In 1912 when she learned that Asquith was to attend a performance at the Theatre Royal, Dublin, Mary Leigh set fire to the stage curtains, threw a burning chair into the orchestra pit and exploded several small bombs. She was a close and lifelong friend of Emily Davison and on another occasion she, Davison and Constance Lytton were arrested for throwing

The WSPU Fife and Drum Band led by Drum Major Mary Leigh.
(Note the age of most of the performers.)

stones at Lloyd George on his way to a meeting in Newcastle. The stones were wrapped in paper bearing the message: *"Rebellion against tyrants is obedience to God."* Mary was imprisoned, went on hunger strike and suffered force feeding on several occasions. Later, like Sarah and many others, she became disillusioned with Emmeline and Christabel Pankhurst's autocratic rule of the WSPU. She therefore transferred her allegiance to Sylvia's 'East London Federation' under whose auspices she continued her activities until the outbreak of war.

She was with Emily Davison when she died in June 1913 at the Epsom Cottage Hospital and later, at the mortuary, she placed in Emily's hands a copy of '*Song of the Open Road*', a book of verse by Walt Whitman, which

Emily Davison's grave at Morpeth, Northumberland.

had been given to her by Lady Constance Lytton. The book was open at one of Emily's favourite poems. She also placed one of Emily's suffragette medals with its force feeding clasps in the coffin.

Mary Leigh acquired the two flags which Emily Davison had pinned inside her coat when she ran onto the racecourse and sustained the injuries which would result in her death. Many people believe it was her intention to attach one of them to the King's horse.

In June 1916 Sarah Benett organised what was to become an annual pilgrimage to the grave of Emily Davison in Morpeth, Northumberland. Mary Leigh attended draped in one of the flags and is said to have made the same pilgrimage each year well into old age. It is also believed that she attended the first 'Campaign for Nuclear Disarmament' (CND) Aldermaston March in 1958 draped in the same flag though it is hard to understand how two women who had themselves eschewed no form of violence in pursuit of their aims, including the use of bombs in public places, would have aligned themselves with the objectives of that organisation.

Though Sarah's militant activities were constrained by the wartime 'truce' her resentment and ambitions were not dimmed and she considered that militancy was only postponed and would resume again after the war:

> *"My militancy divides into two periods and may be called the period of advertising our claim and the period of wrath and retribution for the methods employed against us – methods of fraud and cynicism. The one culminated in the long, patient*

picketting of Parliament – a sacrifice of self which mattered little to the Government; the other is only in abeyance on account of the war and has caused quite a considerable amount of alarm and discomfort to the men in office and the general public." [2]

But it was not to be. Sarah conserved her martial zeal throughout the war years waiting for the battle for women's suffrage to resume, unaware that the heady days of militant sisterhood were over and that the selfless way in which women from all social classes were to come forward to undertake jobs normally done by men, some of them skilled, some of them dangerous, would claim greater success in advancing the cause of women than any previous action.

12. Final Victory

July 1914

The initial confidence in a quick victory and the boys being *'Home by Christmas'* was soon dispelled. Britain, following a decade of Liberal government, had entered the war grossly under-manned and under-funded: Germany had a total of 93 divisions, Russia had 146, France had 73 and the 'British Expeditionary Force', famously described by the Kaiser as *"Britain's contemptible little army"*, had 6 infantry divisions and one cavalry brigade! The blood sacrifice of young British soldiers, as ever demanded by governments which neglect their armed services in times of peace, was duly made and the war soon settled down to a static stalemate of trench warfare stretching from the Channel to the Swiss border.

As the government realised that there could be no quick victory and military leaders struggled to find a way to break the deadlock, it became evident that massive numbers of men and massive quantities of munitions would be necessary. Britain's sacrificed professional army was gradually replaced by Kitchener's hastily-trained volunteers and, eventually, by conscripted men.

Unprecedented volumes of casualties drained Britain of service-aged men leaving huge vacancies in manufacturing and service industries which could only be filled by women of whom there was now a preponderance. The most pressing need was for an unending supply of munitions and war matériel and shell factories were soon being staffed almost entirely by women to provide the enormous quantities of shells required to service the constant artillery bombardments which had become a feature of the static war.

Woman driving a trolley in a munitions factory.

Women at work in a shell filling factory in Chilwell, Nottinghamshire.

Thousands of women, whose pre-war employment opportunities had generally been restricted to domestic service, volunteered for work in the munitions factories. Their pay was much higher than that to which they were accustomed but the hours were long and the work was heavy and hazardous. There were several serious explosions in shell factories in the course of the war with heavy loss of life.

The work was also unhealthy often with poor ventilation and inadequate protective measures. The faces and hands of women who handled the yellow TNT powder which filled the shells became stained with the pigment and the women were commonly known as the 'canaries'.

By the end of the war there was something approaching a million women working in the munitions factories. They had experienced a way of life vastly different from what they had been used to and it had given them a new-found self-confidence and awareness of their own worth. They had played an important part in winning the war and would not be content with returning to the confinement of their pre-war roles.

WOMEN DOING MEN'S JOBS DURING THE WAR.

Top left: **Women took over as conductors in buses and trams.**

Top right: **A woman undertaking the extremely skilled job of shaping an aircraft propeller.**

Below: **The huge communities of women working in factories necessitated the formation of female police contingents.**

Thousands of women saw active service in France and Belgium as nurses in the field hospitals and as ambulance drivers. The above group were working from the enormous British base at Etaples in which there were seventeen military and Red Cross hospitals.

As the war progressed the enormous number of casualties was changing the national ratio of men to women which was causing some concern to those politicians opposed to women's suffrage. If women were granted the vote on the same terms as men, they would actually outnumber men – a situation which had to be guarded against at all costs!

Public opinion, however, was moving steadily towards a sympathetic understanding of the suffragists' demands. The annoyances of the pre-war militancy were soon forgotten and the public developed a new-found respect for the legions of women who were holding the home front together in skilled and semi-skilled jobs of which they had previously been thought incapable.

It was recognised by all political parties that the qualifications for the right to vote would have to be radically changed and an all-party committee, from both Houses of Parliament, and chaired by the Speaker, was established to debate the question. Although the Conference convened in November 1916, the Speaker, Sir James Lowther, whose ruling in 1913 had effectively killed the *Franchise and Registration Bill*, adroitly manipulated the agenda so that votes for women were not discussed until January 1917 after three anti-women's suffrage members of the Committee had been replaced by three who were in sympathy with it. Consequently, it was agreed by an informal vote of 15 to 6 that some measure of women's suffrage should be introduced although the proposal that qualifications for women should be the same as for men was defeated; women acquiring a substantial majority of the electorate could not be entertained. After much discussion it was agreed that a recommendation should go forward that women over the age of 30, subject to certain qualifications, should be given the vote. It was not perfect but it was progress.

A prominent voice for women's rights at the Conference was Millicent Fawcett, leader of the 'National Union of Women's Suffrage Societies' (NUWSS) who had been steering a delicate course between the conflicting pacifist and war-supporting factions of her Union. Regarding the outcome of the 'Speaker's Conference' she said:

> *"We would greatly prefer an imperfect scheme that can pass to the most perfect scheme in the world that could not pass."*
> (41)

She also brought to the attention of the Conference the anomaly of a young man of 19, old enough to fight and die for his country but not old enough to vote. This, also, would need to be addressed in the legislation to come.

The NUWSS never stopped campaigning for women's rights throughout the war and in March 1917 Millicent Fawcett led a deputation of suffragists to the Prime Minister, David Lloyd George, who had replaced the hated Herbert Henry Asquith in December 1916. Lloyd George, despite his brushes with militants in the past, was basically sympathetic to women's suffrage and promised a far more tolerant political climate than his predecessor.

The recommendations of the 'Speaker's Conference' culminated in the *Representation of the People Act* which received Royal Assent in February 1918. The case for significant electoral reform was overwhelming and there

Sir George Cave, later Viscount Cave, Home Secretary 1916-1919

PHOTO BY B VERNARDI OF PORTRAIT BY W R SYMONDS

was very little disagreement between the political parties. The franchise was extended to all men over 21, or 19 if they had military service, and women over 30 with minimal status qualifications. This tripled the electorate from 7.7 million in 1912 to 21.4 million in 1918, 43% of whom were women. The Bill was passed through the Commons with a majority of 385 to 55 in June 1917.

The words of the Home Secretary, Sir George Cave, expressed what those on both sides of the House already knew – that the war had changed everything and the country could never return to the old culture of social exclusion:

"War by all classes of our countrymen has brought us nearer together, has opened men's eyes, and removed misunderstandings on all sides. It has made it, I think, impossible that ever again, at all events in the lifetime of the present generation, there should be a revival of the old class feeling which was responsible for so much, and, among other things, for the exclusion for a period, of so many of our population from the class of electors. I think I need say no more to justify this extension of the franchise." [42]

Trouble was expected in the House of Lords, however, where there was a significant number of members opposed to votes for women. The leader of the House was George Nathaniel Curzon, Earl Curzon of Kedeston, a formidable figure who had served as Viceroy of India from 1899-1905. He was a brilliant and decisive politician but was also a man of extraordinary arrogance who was famously uninformed of the ways of the world outside his own privileged coterie. He believed that: *"the best work in the world*

Lord Curzon, (while Viceroy of India), President of the National League for Opposing Woman Suffrage.

was always done by members of the aristocracy" and, on one occasion, is recorded as saying: *"I never knew that the lower classes had such white skins".* His views on suffrage for women were therefore fairly predictable.

He had spoken strongly in 1914 against the rights of those women who were already allowed to vote in local elections being extended to parliamentary elections. He was Joint President, with Lord Weardale, of the 'National League for Opposing Woman Suffrage' (NLOWS) and those members of the House of Lords who would oppose the electoral changes looked to him to represent their views. But Lord Curzon, recognising the change in public opinion as manifested in the Commons vote, decided not to oppose the will of the people and accepted the inevitable. Deprived of his leadership, support for sabotaging the Bill simply fizzled out and it was passed in the Upper House by 134 to 71. The NLOWS was doomed and its publication *'The Anti Suffrage Review'* never appeared again.

In November 1918 the war came to an end and at the General Election which followed one month later, the new electoral system came into effect. In the same month the *Parliament (Qualification of Women Act) 1918* gave women over 21 years of age the right to stand for election to Parliament; 17 women, including Christabel Pankhurst, sought election but only one was successful – Constance Markievicz, the Sinn Féin candidate for Dublin St. Patrick's, who decided to sit in the Irish Parliament rather than take her seat at Westminster. The first female Member of Parliament to sit at Westminster was Nancy Astor in 1919.

Also in 1919 Sarah moved from Hampstead to a house in Village Road, Finchley where she was to remain for the rest of her life. She now had the vote; the battle had, at least in part, been won and she must have felt considerable fulfilment that the hard and health damaging work she had voluntarily undertaken for twelve years had not been in vain. Her hopes for a renewal of militancy after the war were finished and, being a very intelligent woman, she must have been impressed by the progress towards equality made, almost unintentionally, by women whose motivation had simply been to help the war effort and advance their own personal expectations rather than campaign for women's rights. She must also have wondered to what extent these changes might have come about naturally through the demands of the war economy without the sacrifices which she and her suffragette sisters had made. It was a question which was pondered on by many ex-suffragettes and which still creates lively debate today.

Later in life Sarah believed that her decision to become a suffragette had come from a force within herself and was not the result of influence by those people and events around her:

"When my home life came to an end, I fixed on the Potteries as my home and I was there 12 years later, when, in 1906, the militant suffrage movement began; but I am firmly convinced

'Norton' the house in Village Road, Finchley, where Sarah lived for the last five years of her life.

ADRIAN RICHARDSON

that those of us who have been resolutely and persistently militant, got our inspiration, not from any Movement, but from ourselves – from the life influences which had been moulding us to be rebels. People become rebels when they see that it is the only way to save themselves and others from being vic[timised] . . ." [2]

In her final years, Sarah was reconciled, to some extent, with at least some branches of her family. When her eldest brother, William Charles Benett, retired from the Bengal Civil Service he bought a house, 'Oatlands', just outside the Oxfordshire village of Warborough. Sarah is thought to have lived with him there for a time, possibly between her residencies in Hampstead and Finchley. Her crippled brother Newton also lived with Charles at Oatlands from where he continued his painting in a part of the house which was ideally lit for a studio. Newton died in 1914 and William

'Oatlands', Warborough, home of William Charles Benett with whom Sarah lived for a time. The multi-windowed wing at the top of the house served as Newton Benett's studio.

AUTHOR 2017

in 1922 and both are buried in the churchyard of St. Laurence, Warborough. William left the house to his niece, Mary Knyfton Leathes, who was separated from her husband and lived with her four children. One of these, Edward ('Teddy') de Mussenden Leathes, wrote in 1994:

> *"When we knew Aunt Sarah, she was living with her brother, Uncle Willie, at a house called "Oatlands", Warborough, Oxon, and at one time Uncle Newton also lived there . . . it was a large, rambling house with six bedrooms, four servants' bedrooms and a gardener's cottage . . . on one side of the garden there stretched over a mile of cornfields with Dorchester Abbey just beyond. So you can imagine my mother's delight at being left such a property . . ."* [43]

Teddy's younger sister, Ivy, the only member of the family who was a beneficiary in Sarah's Will, also recalled Sarah in 1994:

> *"Re. Aunt Sarah, I'm afraid I know very little. She did take me to my first theatre – none other than 'King Lear', hardly the right choice for a young schoolgirl!! She also left me a little money to have when I reached 21 years. It seemed a long way off when I suppose I was about 13 or 14. As my brothers and I were at boarding schools from about the ages of 8 and 9, we really heard very little about the great aunts and uncles."* [44]

Ivy was twice married and became a Justice of the Peace. Their brother Reggie rose to the rank of major-general and became Colonel-Commandant of the Royal Marines in 1975. Teddy spent most of his working life in South America, was married in 1941 and died in 2002 at the age of 91. 'Oatlands' was sold in 1938 following the death of Mary Leathes from dysentery while on holiday in Cyprus and, having been used as a nursing home for a time, is now divided into nine flats.

Sarah had also remained in contact with her niece, Constance Augusta Burlton Allen with whom she had spent much time when the family lived

**The wedding in 1904 of Constance Augusta Burlton Allen
to Charles Hugh Purvis. Sarah is third from the right in the back row**

in Lyme Regis. Constance had apparently forgiven her for scaring the life out of her with her reckless driving of the pony trap and for making her walk home in the rain in her evening dress! In 1904 Constance married Charles Hugh Purvis, great-grandson of the famous Admiral John Child Purvis, and Sarah attended the wedding.

Sarah also left the account of her imprisonments and her *Cat & Mouse* documents to Constance with the following hand-written inscription:

> *"'My Imprisonments'(MS) and my three licenses should be kept by Constance and her children as an heirloom and record of what helped to win the vote."* [2]

They are still in the hands of Constance's descendants.

Having worked incessantly throughout the war years for a number of voluntary organisations where her enthusiasm and organising skills could be of use, Sarah lived quietly in her house in the leafy suburb of Finchley

222

for the last few years until her death on 4th February 1924 aged 74. The cause of death recorded on her Death Certificate is 'Pernicious Anaemia' which in 1924 probably meant straight B12 deficiency which could have been caused by poor diet and the periodic disturbances to her system during imprisonments and hunger strikes. It is not known if Sarah was a vegetarian but if, like many suffragettes, she was, this might well have contributed to her condition.

The 29th February 1924 edition of '*The Vote*', the newspaper of the 'Women's Freedom League', featured on its front page a handsome tribute to its erstwhile Honorary Treasurer, under the heading:

"Sarah Benett, Fighter, Friend and Comrade"

"Sarah Benett came of a distinguished family, was highly educated and cultured, delighting in beauty in every form, country life and travel; of strong personality, keen intellect, entirely without fear, she was simple and direct in her methods, never hesitating, but gladly and cheerfully giving all that she had at the call of the helpless and oppressed. All her life greatly interested in education, she served on local educational bodies in the Potteries with a passion for justice, mercy and pity, her sympathies were very wide, especially for women, children and animals, and she was an impressive speaker and clear writer." [45]

The article then details her protests, arrests and imprisonments leading up to her final hunger strike when she was threatened with forcible feeding but finally released. It concludes:

"These hardships, and overwork during the war, broke down her health. Death, the friend, came to her, but we grieve for the loss of her always ready help, and shall miss from our gathering her fine face, instinct with cheery, kindly humour."
[45]

Sarah's Will contained legacies to several interesting people. She appointed as her executors John Rose, a Pall Mall solicitor, and Dr. Elizabeth Wilks to whom she also left £250 *[£14,250 today]*.

Elizabeth Wilks was a friend of Sarah's, a committed suffragette and an enthusiastic member of the 'Woman's Tax Resistance League'. As a doctor of medicine, she had an income sufficient to make her liable to income tax which she refused to pay. In 1913 this had given rise to a bizarre situation which invoked questions in Parliament and attracted media attention throughout the country. In English law a man could be imprisoned for his wife's failure to pay her taxes and this is exactly what happened – her unfortunate husband, Mark Wilks, was taken off and thrown into jail without any attempt by his wife to help him.

This became known as 'The Wilks Affair' and caused widespread disbelief and outrage. The Tory press seized the opportunity to ridicule the Liberal government over its ineptitude and a great protest meeting was held in London in October, presided over by Sir John Cockburn. The principal speaker, George Bernard Shaw said:

"I knew of cases in my boyhood where women managed to make homes for their children and themselves, and then the husbands sold the furniture, turned the wife and children out, and got drunk. The Married Woman's Property Act was then carried, under which the husband retained the responsibility of the property, and the wife had the property to herself. As Mrs. Wilks would not pay the tax on her own income Mr. Wilks went to jail. If my wife did that to me, the very moment I came out of prison I would get another wife. It is indefensible." [46]

George Bernard Shaw in 1915

NEW YORK TIMES

The novelist Israel Zangwill, who had always been a supporter of the suffrage movement, introduced a note of levity to the meeting by suggesting that, under this legislation, a man marrying an heiress could be securing his own ruin.

Wilks was released from prison after a few weeks, an effective admission by the government that it had been a mistake to imprison him in the first place. '*The Times*' leader pointed out the anomalies and changing balance of advantage in the law concerning husbands and wives:

> "*From one extreme the law has gone to another. The husband is liable for the wrongs committed by his wife, though he has no power to prevent her from committing them. She for many kinds of contracts is his agent, and can bind him practically to almost any amount. He may be compelled to find her in funds wherewith to carry on proceedings in the Divorce Court. Liabilities founded upon the identity of husband and wife are continued when, by reason of the Married Woman's Property Acts, it no longer exists. Of these anomalies we rarely hear, though, as any one conversant with proceedings in Courts of Law is aware, they lead to cases quite as hard as that of Mr. Wilks. Somehow, then, is kept well in the background the fact that, in a Parliament elected by men, laws placing them in a position of inferiority and disadvantage are passed.*" (47)

A small legacy of £25 *[£1,425 today]* was included for Edith Margaret Garrud, described as a 'Physical Culture Instructor'. In fact, she was the woman who had gained fame during the militant suffragette days by teaching them jiu-jitsu. Garrud and her husband, William, who was also a boxing and physical training instructor, learned jiu-jitsu from the Japanese exponent of the art, Sadakazu Uyenishi, at his School of Japanese Self Defence at 31 Golden Square, Soho. When Uyenishi returned to Japan in 1908, the Garruds took over the school with Edith responsible for training women and children.

THE SUFFRAGETTE THAT KNEW JIU-JITSU.

THE ARREST.

A cartoon in *Punch* showing a jiu-jitsu-trained member of the WSPU 'Bodyguard' holding off a squad of terrified policemen!

In 1913 the WSPU appointed 30 able-bodied women to form a 'bodyguard', partly for the protection of their leaders and partly to protect women who had been released from prison under the *Cat and Mouse Act* from being hounded for re-arrest when their period of freedom had expired. This bodyguard was trained in jiu-jitsu by Edith Garrud in secret locations to avoid police intervention; she also instructed them in the use of Indian clubs which started to appear on the more violent demonstrations and were used alongside the jiu-jitsu with considerable skill by the athletic women of the bodyguard.

Sarah at the age of 63 was obviously too old to be a member of the bodyguard but undoubtedly approved of its activities. She certainly knew and kept in touch with Edith Garrud who was a witness to a codicil which Sarah added to her Will four months before her death.

Sarah also left a legacy of £30 *[£1,710 today]* to the Countess de Vismes. Born Bede Dalley, daughter of an Australian barrister, this larger-than-life lady had led a colourful career. Brought up in London, Sydney and

Bohemian Paris, where she lived with an aunt who was a painter, Bede was married in London in 1917 to Count Alexander de Vismes de Pontieu, whose aristocratic French family had settled in England in the 17th century.

The couple went to live in Santiago, Chile, but after four years Bede left her husband and returned to London, penniless, where she was employed in a variety of jobs including hop picker, chambermaid, charwoman and waitress in a milk bar. She was obviously a strong willed and mercurial woman who it is easy to suppose might also have been a militant suffragette.

Gertrude Toynbee received £25 *[£1,425 today]*. She was involved in many charities and associations including the 'Committee for the Relief of Russian Exiles in Russia and Siberia' of which she was the Honorary Secretary. She was also a suffragist, though not of the militant kind, and had on one occasion written to '*The Times*' to disassociate herself and her friends from the rowdy behaviour of her militant colleagues.

Sarah's housekeeper, Marian Swinscoe, received £25 *[£1,425 today]* as did Margaret Waring, a cousin on her mother's side. As previously mentioned, her only other relative to receive a bequest was her great-niece, Ivy Leathes to whom she left £1,000 to be paid to her upon reaching the age of 25 or on her marriage. This, in today's terms, was a legacy of £57,000, a considerable sum by any standard, and it is rather sad that the beneficiary should have apparently dismissed it so lightly: "*She also left me a little money . . .*" Had she forgotten, one wonders, the munificence of her bequest? One gets the impression that she did not wholly approve of her great-aunt Sarah in spite of the attention she received from her. Sarah had five nephews/nieces and eight great-nephews/nieces but Ivy Leathes was the only one of them to receive her favours. The probate value of Sarah's estate was £7,344 *[£418,608 today]* and her largest bequest of £2,000 *[£114,000 today]* was to the National Trust for places of Historic Interest or Natural Beauty. However, the Will stated that if, after payment of her various pecuniary bequests, there should remain a residue, this should be added to the bequest of £1,000 *[£57,000]* to the 'Elizabeth Garrett Anderson Hospital for Women'. In the event, there was a surplus of £1,844 so the Hospital received a total of £2,844 *[£162,108 today]* – an extremely handsome endowment.

The New Hospital for Women which in 1918 was renamed
The Elizabeth Garrett Anderson Hospital, the principal beneficiary in Sarah's Will.

The Hospital had started life as 'Saint Mary's Dispensary' which cared for poor and needy women and children in Central London who could not afford to pay for medical attention. In 1890 it became the 'New Hospital for Women' and in 1918 was renamed the 'Elizabeth Garrett Anderson Hospital for Women' in honour of its co-founder and physician who had given it 20 years of devoted service and had died in the previous year.

Elizabeth's almost unbelievable struggle to become a qualified doctor illustrates perfectly the debilitating gender inequality which faced ambitious women in those days. Determined to study medicine, all the applications she initially made were rejected and she eventually enrolled as a nurse at the Middlesex Hospital from which position she lobbied constantly for admission to the hospital's medical school. She was eventually allowed to undertake certain studies and attend some of the lectures but her male fellow students resented the presence of a woman in their midst and conspired to have her thrown out. She then applied for admission to the medical schools of Oxford, Cambridge, Edinburgh, Glasgow and St. Andrews and was rejected by them all.

Elizabeth then decided to enter the profession through the back door and was admitted to the 'Worshipful Society of Apothecaries' whose constitution did not allow them to reject women on grounds of gender. After intensive private study and tutorials with a number of leading professors, she eventually sat and passed the examination of the 'Society of Apothecaries' and obtained a licence to practise medicine though, as a woman, she was not allowed to work in any hospital. (The Apothecaries then amended their constitution so they would not be compelled to admit further women in the future!)

Elizabeth, at the age of 29, then started her own practice at 20 Upper Berkeley Street and six months later opened the 'St. Mary's Dispensary' at 69 Seymour Place. A major outbreak of cholera in 1866, which demanded the involvement of every form and level of medical assistance that could be mustered, temporarily anaesthetised the objections of the authorities to

A caricature of Elizabeth Garrett Anderson as the first female member of the London School Board.

WELLCOME IMAGES

her new venture and eased her acceptance into the male dominated world of medicine.

Upon learning that the Faculty of Medicine at the Sorbonne in Paris was accepting female students, she learnt French so she could take the medical examinations in France. She passed and at last obtained her medical degree allowing her to practise medicine wherever she wished. In the same year she became the first woman to be elected to the 'London School Board' to which she made a major contribution.

In 1873 Elizabeth gained membership of the 'British Medical Association'. The BMA, like the Apothecaries, immediately changed their membership rules to prevent the admission of any further women for another 19 years; but she had got her foot in the door of two exclusively male establishments creating a precedent for those who followed her.

This remarkable woman was the first female to qualify as a doctor in both Britain and France, the founder of the first hospital for women, staffed by women and dealing with women's conditions, the founder of the first medical school for women, which became the famous 'Royal Free', and its first Dean, the first elected female member of the London School Board and, as mayor of her home town of Aldeburgh in Suffolk, the first female mayor and magistrate in Britain.

Elizabeth Garrett Anderson died in December 1917 and the following year the 'New Hospital for Women' was renamed the 'Elizabeth Garrett Anderson Hospital' in her honour. Today, the unit lives on as the 'Elizabeth Garrett Anderson Wing of University College Hospital', a major teaching hospital on the Euston Road in Fitzrovia.

Rebel with a Cause

For Sarah Bennet, who had dedicated her life to the advancement and acceptance of women, to the breaking down of the barriers of ignorance and prejudice which had kept women subjected and excluded for so long, there was perhaps no institution with a better claim upon her beneficence and no person whose memory was more worthy of perpetuation than Elizabeth Garrett Anderson.

A ward in the 'New Hospital for Women' c.1899.

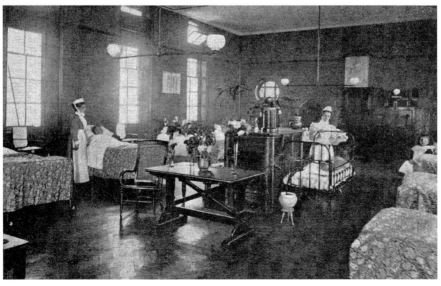

13. Militancy – Help or Hindrance?

2nd July 1928

On 2nd July 1928 the *Representation of the People (Equal Franchise) Act* became law and at last, after the years of struggle, women acquired electoral equality with men. Now all citizens over 21, male and female, were entitled to vote regardless of their status or ownership of property.

Sadly, it was too late for Sarah to see, though she had herself enjoyed the vote for the last six years of her life, and it was also too late for Mrs. Emmeline Pankhurst who died on 2nd July, two weeks before it became law, though she had been aware of the Bill's introduction in March.

It was not, however, too late for Millicent Fawcett, longtime leader of the non-militant suffragists and now a 'Dame Grand Cross of the Order of the British Empire'. She was in the House of Commons to see the historic vote take place and later wrote:

> *"It is almost exactly 61 years ago since I heard John Stuart Mill introduce his suffrage amendment to the Reform Bill on 20 May 1867. So I have had extraordinary good luck in having seen the struggle from the beginning."* [48]

Since 1906 when Charles Hanley of the *'Daily Mail'* had coined the mildly contemptuous word 'Suffragette' for a militant suffragist, a clear breach had existed between those advocating peaceful but persistent action within the law and those who had tried law abiding means with no success and saw militancy as the only means to achieve their ends. As Sarah Benett had written:

> *"We had come to see how worse than futile it was to do easy things to get the vote – that we were up against a calm, indulgent cynicism."* [2]

ORIGIN AND DEVELOPMENT OF A SUFFRAGETTE.

At 15 a little Pet.

At 20 a little Coquette

At 40 not married yet!

At 50 A Suffragette.

VOTES FOR WOMEN

"THE WEEK"

An example of the many cruel cartoons which pilloried the suffragettes.

And on the surface, it would certainly have seemed that the peaceful agitation of the early suffragists had brought about no progress whatever. Numerous petitions and representations had gone before Parliament, Members had been continuously lobbied, women's suffrage had been debated, bills introduced, some of which received a second reading, but all had been rejected. In 1905 when militant action started, it appeared that nearly 40 years of peaceful, law-abiding action had achieved nothing.

Then, in the early days of militancy when action was limited to aggressive marching, slogan shouting and knocking off policemen's helmets, the militants enjoyed tacit support from their non-militant sisters. Speaking of the suffragettes in 1906 Millicent Fawcett wrote:

> *"I hope the more old fashioned suffragists will stand by them. In my opinion, far from having injured the movement [they] have done more during the last twelve months to bring it within the region of practical politics than we have been able to accomplish in the same number of years."* [49]

They also enjoyed a degree of sympathy from the general public though the majority attitude was of ridicule and mild amusement as was illustrated in the rash of contemptuous cartoons which portrayed suffragettes as shrieking harpies, ugly middle-aged women who had failed to find a husband or irresponsible married women who neglected their families and their homes. In fact, this was far from the case; the majority of suffragettes were married women and many, such as Mrs. Pankhurst and her daughters, and Annie Kenney, were very attractive.

What cannot be denied is that the behaviour of the militants attracted far more publicity and public awareness than that of their non-violent colleagues; but the NUWSS, led by their President, Millicent Fawcett, worked away incessantly in the background and their measured and reasonable canvassing of influential politicians undoubtedly sowed seeds which would later bear fruit. The 'split' in 1907 and the formation of the WFL was purely due to the Pankhursts' autocratic management of the WSPU and had nothing to do with the censure of militancy; hence the return of Sarah and other like-minded activists to the WSPU after they had made their protest.

In 1912 everything changed. With the collapse of the new *Conciliation Bill* in November 1911 the anger and frustration of WSPU members erupted into an escalation of violence involving the destruction and vandalism of public and private property. Sarah wholeheartedly approved of this but the law-abiding moderates hastened to disassociate themselves from such actions. The NUWSS saw such progress as they had made with recruiting support at Westminster now jeopardised by the new wave of violence. Millicent Fawcett later wrote:

> *"Militants were the chief obstacles in the way of success of the suffrage movement in the House of Commons."* [50]

Later in the year, the expulsion of the Pethick-Lawrences from the WSPU lost the Union two of its erstwhile greatest supporters and a voice of moderation and reason which had earned considerable respect with the public for whom, in the main, the new violence had gone too far; it was one thing to turn a blind eye to the breaking of a few shop windows, it was quite another thing to condone the blowing up of pillar boxes, the destruction of national art treasures, the burning down of private property and the physical assault of politicians who did not support their cause. The suffragettes had

Jennie Baines presents a bouquet to Mrs. Emmeline Pethick-Lawrence whose husband is on the extreme left next to Flora Drummond.

won much public sympathy when the brutal details of their treatment in prison, particularly the force feeding, became known, but this sympathy was soon eroded by news of the outrageous acts of vandalism in which the WSPU had become involved.

In Parliament opinion hardened as politicians who previously may have been sympathetic to the suffragists' cause did not wish it to appear that violence had triumphed. In 1913 Lloyd George wrote:

> *"Haven't the suffragettes the sense to see that the very worst way of campaigning for the vote is to try to intimidate a man into giving them what he would gladly give otherwise?"* [51]

Viscount Helmsley, MP for Thirsk and Malton, pointed out that in the Women's Suffrage debate in the House of Commons in March 1912, all the

Charles Duncombe, Viscount Helmsley and later 2nd Earl of Feversham, MP for Thirsk and Malton. He was killed in action in France in 1916 together with his deerhound which was buried with him.

ILLUSTRATED LONDON NEWS 30/9/1916

MPs who were against it gave suffragettes' violence as the main cause of their opposition.

He also drew Members' attention to the fact that, if women were given the vote, it would not be the moderate, law-abiding women who would become involved in politics but:

> " . . . *those very militant women who have brought so much disgrace and discredit upon their sex. It would introduce a disastrous element into our public life.*" [52]

Overall, there can be little doubt that the militant action of WSPU members made the Government more intransigent. By definition, terrorism is *"The unlawful use of violence and intimidation in the pursuit of political aims"*, and many Members of Parliament simply dismissed the WSPU as a terrorist organisation. An article in the *'Morning Post'* of 2nd March 1912 summed up the reaction of many politicians and members of the public to suffragette violence:

> *"Nothing could indicate more plainly their lack of fitness to be entrusted with the exercise of political power."* [53]

It should also be remembered that while the WSPU had eschewed any form of affiliation with any political party, the NUWSS had developed strong links with the emergent Labour Party whose support would be invaluable in their campaign for the 1918 *Representation of the People Act*. This liaison also served to present the NUWSS as champions of the working classes whereas the WSPU, in the perception of many, and despite the large element of industrial workers in their membership, still retained their rather exclusive middle class image.

However, if today one asked ten British people what was the major factor in obtaining the vote for women, nine would undoubtedly say the actions of the suffragettes; and what person was most prominent in the movement? Mrs. Pankhurst; and what events were most notable? Women chaining themselves to the railings of Buckingham Palace and Emily Davison throwing herself in front of the King's horse at Epsom (for that is how her action is commonly perceived). All these were people and actions of the WSPU to which the credit for female suffrage is today clearly attributed in the consciousness of the masses.

This is not surprising as it was the militants and their actions which grabbed the headlines and were recorded in history and folklore. After 40 years of lawful protest since John Stuart Mill presented the first petition for female suffrage to Parliament in 1867, the emergence of the suffragettes and their militant actions breathed new life into the movement and brought it to the attention of people who had never before considered it. For the first time it became a public issue, a status it would never have achieved until the First World War without the dramatic endeavours of the suffragettes.

The war, of course, introduced a new element to the debate. The suffragettes were effectively disbanded, many volunteering for war service, and their pre-war activities were soon lost sight of with the emergence of the new roles and responsibilities of women in the wartime economy. Some will argue that it was this alone which secured the vote for women and it was certainly a convenient proposition for those uncompromising, anti-suffrage politicians who could now dismiss half a century of campaigning by dedicated women as inconsequential. In truth, the war was a very significant factor in redressing one of the greatest injustices in modern history, not just with politicians but with members of the public who saw women doing men's work, and doing it well. This brought into focus for the first time the gross tyranny of a system which treated women as inferior, second-class citizens – a notion which they had seen regularly vilified by suffragists before the war but which had never really registered with them.

Memorial to Mrs. Emmeline Pankhurst in Victoria Tower Gardens.

So, was militancy a help or a hindrance? A comfortable compromise, which is reasonable and very probably correct, is the view held by many scholars today. This concludes that the WSPU did sterling work in the early days, in gaining publicity for the cause and bringing it to the attention of politicians and public alike, but that, from 1912 to 1914, their actions probably did more damage to their own cause than to the objects of their vandalism.

That Mrs. Pankhurst and her militant suffragettes have taken the credit for women's suffrage in the public's awareness is illustrated by her bronze statue which has stood in Victoria Tower Gardens, next to the Palace of Westminster, since 1930, two years after her death. Only in 2017 was a national statue of Dame Millicent Fawcett commissioned and approved. It was undertaken by Gillian Wearing and depicts Mrs. Fawcett carrying a placard reading: *"Courage calls to Courage everywhere"* – an excerpt from a speech she made at Emily Davison's funeral. The statue, in Parliament Square, was unveiled on 24th April 2018 in the presence of many dignitaries ncluding the Prime Minister and the Mayor of London.

Rebel with a Cause

On the left pier of the Pankhurst memorial is a depiction of the WSPU's Holloway Prison badge, as worn proudly by Sarah, and on the right a profile medallion of Christabel's head with a plaque reading:

"These Walls and Piers have been erected in Memory of Dame Christabel Pankhurst who jointly with her mother Mrs. Emmeline Pankhurst inspired and led the militant suffrage campaign."

On the outbreak of war in 1914, Christabel, who had stayed with Sarah at her house in Burslem, returned from exile and redirected her immense drive and passion into campaigning for military conscription and the internment of enemy nationals. She toured the country with Norah Dacre Fox, another ex WSPU militant, lecturing and handing out white feathers, the symbol of cowardice, to any young men she came across who were not in uniform. In the 1918 General Election she stood unsuccessfully for Parliament then emigrated to America where she then turned her passion towards Christian evangelism and became a leading member of the Second Adventist movement. In 1936 she was created a Dame Commander of the Order of the British Empire. It is interesting that Christabel, the most militant member of the family, received an honour which was denied her more prominent mother and her very much more moderate sisters.

Sylvia Pankhurst, whose political views had diverged fundamentally from those of her mother and sisters, was fervently against the war and moved steadily to the left eventually founding the Communist Workers Party. In 1927, at the age of 45, Sylvia who was living with an Italian anarchist, had an illegitimate child by him which caused her mother to break all ties with her. It is said that this broke her mother's heart and she died soon after.

Sylvia Pankhurst c.1910

Sarah Benett's rebellion against her own social class, and her family's upper-middle class mores, did not occur until after her parents' death so her inheritance was not prejudiced. It did, however, cause a complete estrangement with her siblings and their children for most of her life as an active suffragette.

After the war, however, there seems to have been a gradual thawing of bad feeling. She stayed for a time with her eldest brother William at his house in Oxfordshire and may also have been in contact with her youngest brother Newton, the artist, before his death in 1914. She certainly had contact with her niece Constance Purvis (née Allen), whom she had known well during her days in Lyme Regis, as she left her the manuscript she had written. She was also in touch with her great-niece Ivy Leathes, the only relative remembered in her Will.

It is probable, and sincerely to be hoped, that as the years went by, the shame her family felt in her rebellious lifestyle may gradually have turned to pride as they recognised her courage and the commitment which had driven her. In a note attached to her prison memoirs she wrote:

> *"I am one of a large family and, in some ways, I have lived seriously from early years. I dare not say what, looking back, I feel to be the events which have tended to make me a militant suffragette, partly because I cannot do this without mentioning others, partly because I have, anyhow, to say too much about myself. I have to make statements which give the impression that I have a high opinion of myself, but I should like to say once for all that . . ."* [2]

and here Sarah stopped as if considering how best to reassure whoever might read her notes in the future that it had not been her intention to portray herself as anything other than an unimportant observer of events. Yet she had, in middle age, for a principle in which she passionately believed, exposed herself to mob violence on the streets, suffered the indignity of repeated arrests and the discomfort of repeated imprisonments with the damage to her health which this law-defying lifestyle had caused. And how, without relating her part in them, could she have recorded the events she had witnessed and in which she had taken part?

Her modesty, it seems, would not allow her to find a sufficiently self-effacing way of expressing what she was trying to convey so, after several crossings out, she simply wrote:

"I have done my best for the cause." [2]

And who could argue with that?

14. Closure

It is difficult to assess whether Sarah's efforts in educational reform made any real difference in the Potteries but her ideas certainly provided some food for thought with progressive educators and for ridicule with the more conservative and inflexible officials who, one fears, probably constituted a majority at that time.

The lead she set in co-operative trading, also, though sadly unrecorded and uncredited, must certainly have assisted in locally kick-starting the movement which, in October 1917, was to erupt with the formation of the Co-operative Party at a meeting in Central Hall, Westminster. Today the Co-operative Group in the UK, owned by its four million members, has 4,200 outlets and employs around 60,000 people. The fact that Sarah was a woman would have exempted her from any modest share in the credit, of course.

There is no denying, however, her success in the realms of health and safety in the potbanks and among the potters' wives and children. Throughout her eleven years in the Potteries, she nagged away at these issues in spite of a lack of concern from the authorities and, often, a lack of co-operation from the trades unions whose interests were, after all, the object of her endeavours. Again, she was a woman and not to be taken seriously. It must have been manifestly dispiriting yet she kept at it year after year. It is little wonder that, in the end, she reached the conclusion that there could be no progress in the status of women until they had the vote and that the fight to obtain it must be her number one priority.

Her greatest success was, perhaps, in bringing to public attention the need for urgent reform of regulations and practices concerning workers exposed to hazardous substances – particularly lead, which was killing hundreds of men and women engaged in the glazing process.

Sarah started her agitation with a letter to the *'Daily Chronicle'* which she followed up with intensive enquiries into health risks in the potbanks. She passed on her findings to the Duchess of Sutherland who shared her concern for workers' health and whose greater public profile gave the matter far wider exposure than Sarah could have achieved on her own. Their joint efforts undoubtedly hastened the government's commissioning of the 1898 'Thorpe-Oliver Enquiry' which concluded that alternatives to lead glazes were now available to manufacturers and which, in turn, set in motion the chain of research and the introduction of increasingly protective measures for workers which led, eventually, to regulations where a failure to operate a workplace to the requisite standard could give rise to criminal liability. Today, the *Control of Lead at Work Regulations 2002* (CLAW) place a duty on employers to prevent, or where this is not reasonably practicable, to control employee exposure to lead and one must claim, on Sarah Benett's behalf, at least a part of the credit for this.

In recent years, many have become wearied by the bizarre and politically correct demands of extreme feminism and may consequently take a palsied view of the suffragettes, and others, who got the movement started. The concept that women were second-class citizens, and could not be trusted in any position of decision-making or authority, was so deeply engraved in the western psyche that it required explosive actions to bring the injustice to the attention of the public and start the debate on the wisdom and morality of this assumption. The suffragettes provided this and the Movement built up an unstoppable momentum without which progress might never have been made. This momentum was so powerful that it continued long after its objectives had been met and, to some extent, continues today when women have reached the top of almost every trade and profession. There are women commanding warships, flying high-speed combat aircraft, commanding troops in the battle line and in the upper echelons of the law, medicine, politics, industry, engineering, education, sport and all creative spheres. Yet there are still extremists who would see the destruction of the nuclear family and the reduction of men to 10 percent of the population. Fortunately these represent a very small minority of women and the suffragettes cannot be held responsible for such impassioned views.

Today, in a society which no longer regards homosexuality as abnormal and no longer requires its practice to remain undercover, much has emerged recently concerning lesbianism among the high-ranking suffragettes and,

Mary Blathwayt (standing) with Annie Kenney and Margaret Hewitt in 1909

although it is not within the remit of this book to examine this subject in any depth, it has to be said that a great deal of it seems to have existed. It was common knowledge within the WSPU that Mrs. Pankhurst had a long-term relationship with Dame Ethel Smyth, the composer, with whom, on occasions, she had shared a cell in Holloway.

The diaries of Mary Blathwayt, whose parents opened Eagle House, their home near Bath, as a retreat for suffragettes in need of rest and tranquillity, reveal the tensions and jealousies within the movement. Annie Kenney, it would appear, was something of a *femme fatale* who captured the hearts of many of her colleagues with some ten of whom she is said to have had love affairs. The most passionate and long-lasting of these was with Christabel Pankhurst and her name was also linked with Emmeline Pethick-Lawrence and Clara Codd.

Teresa Billington-Greig expressed concern that what she described as *"unhealthy emotional attachments"* between members might damage the reputation and credibility of the Movement. She mentioned Christabel

Lovers Annie Kenney and Christabel Pankhurst.

Pankhurst, Emmeline Pethick-Lawrence and Annie Kenney. There were also fears that these attachments might lead to favouritism and imprudent appointments and promotions.

Professor Martin Pugh, biographer of the Pankhursts and a prolific writer and lecturer on social history and the suffrage movement, points out that many biographers tacitly acknowledge the existence of lesbianism among the leaders of the WSPU but skirt diplomatically around the subject. After the First World War the subject was discussed more openly but it is only recently that it has been fully exposed.

Annie Kenney in her 1924 autobiography '*Memories of a Militant*' described how suffragettes lived by a different set of rules and values to other women.

> "*The changed life into which most of us entered was a revolution in itself. No home life, no one to say what we should do or what we should not do, no family ties, we were free and alone in a great brilliant city, scores of young women scarcely out of their teens met together in a revolutionary movement, outlaws or breakers of laws, independent of everything and everybody, fearless and self-confident.*" (54)

The WSPU was an exclusive club which, for young women, offered a lifestyle of close companionship and excitement not unlike that in a girls' boarding school. For Sarah, however, at the age of 60, it must have been difficult at times to endure the high spirits and frivolity within the youthful coterie in which she found herself. They were brave and dedicated women but the subsequent writings of many of them reveal considerable nostalgia for those heady days of confederacy. Sarah Benett never really attained 'management level', apart from her time as Treasurer of the WFL during which her abrasive manner appears to have made her difficult to work with. Most of her time, therefore, was spent among the rank and file which, one feels, may not, on occasions, have provided the intellectual stimulus she sought.

Despite her age, Sarah was physically, as well as mentally, strong. She could never, otherwise, have undertaken the gruelling march from Edinburgh to London in 1912. Her experience with the physical education of her nieces at Lyme Regis stood her in good stead in prison where she took charge of organising games and healthy pursuits for her young companions to the surprise and approval of the prison authorities. One feels, nevertheless, that she must have been rather lonely and isolated for much of her time as a suffragette.

Although militancy ceased in 1914, many of the people with whom Sarah rubbed shoulders in the WSPU and WFL remained in the public eye, some achieving ongoing renown and some falling, or retiring, into obscurity.

All three of the Pankhurst sisters died abroad:

Dame Christabel Pankhurst, who had emigrated to the United States after her narrow defeat in the 1918 General Election, died in California in 1958 aged 77 having devoted the latter years of her life to evangelism and writing and lecturing on the 'Second Coming'. She was unmarried and had never had a relationship with a man.

Sylvia Pankhurst moved away from communism in the 1930s and became involved in anti-fascist organisations. She was also deeply interested in Ethiopia and became a friend of, and adviser to, the Emperor Haile Selassie on whose invitation she moved to Addis Ababa in 1956 with her son Robin. She died in 1960 aged 78 and, as an 'Honorary Ethiopian', received a full

The Holy Trinity Cathedral in Addis Ababa where Sylvia Pankhurst is buried.

state funeral and the honour of being the only foreigner to have been buried in front of the Holy Trinity Cathedral in Addis Ababa.

Adela Pankhurst (Walsh), who had been a founding member of the Communist Party of Australia, also turned her back on communism and in 1927 founded the anti-communist 'Australian Women's Guild of Empire' and later the right wing 'Australia First Movement'. She married Tom Walsh a Trades Union Official and produced one son and five daughters. She died in Sydney in 1961 aged 75.

Frederick Pethick-Lawrence, after his ignominious dismissal from the WSPU, had a distinguished career in politics and was ennobled in 1945. His wife, **Emmeline**, died in 1954 aged 86. Lord Pethick-Lawrence married again and died in 1961 aged 89.

Flora McKinnon Drummond, 'The General', was divorced and remarried in 1922 and was a pall bearer at the funeral of Emmeline Pankhurst in 1928. Two years later she founded the 'Women's Guild of Empire' which opposed communism and fascism. She died in 1949 aged 70.

Annie Kenney joined Emmeline Pankhurst, Flora Drummond and others in support of the war and travelled around the country to encourage trades unions to support war work. She died of diabetes in 1953 aged 73.

Charlotte Despard, elder stateswoman of the WFL, refused, as a pacifist, to support the war, to the embarrassment of her brother Field Marshal Sir John French. Moving steadily towards the political left, she eventually joined the 'Communist Party of Great Britain' and 'Friends of Soviet Russia' and died in 1939, still politically active at the age of 95. Having supported the Republican movement in Ireland, she was buried in a Republican cemetery in Dublin.

Lady Harberton, who led Sarah's first march on Westminster in 1907, died in 1911 and is best remembered for her work on cycling for women and the introduction of 'Rational Dress' – a more suitable attire when riding a bicycle than a long riding habit. As with so many other advances in women's affairs, 'Rationals', as the knickerbocker suits were called, took a long time to be accepted by the more conservative members of society.

Teresa Billington-Greig, one of the founders of the WFL, became a prolific writer of books and articles and remained active in women's affairs right up to her death in 1964. After the Second World War she became involved with several women's groups including the 'Six Point Group' pressing for satisfactory legislation and for equality for women in a number of areas.

Marion Wallace Dunlop, the suffragette who introduced the tactic of hunger striking, and was the first to be force fed in prison, remained true to the cause and was also a pall bearer at Emmeline Pankhurst's funeral. She then took over the care of Mrs. Pankhurst's adopted daughter Mary.

Lady Constance Bulwer-Lytton died in 1923 at the age of 54 following a heart attack very possibly the result of her lifestyle and imprisonments. Raised in India, where her father was Viceroy, she had rejected her background and never married as her mother would not permit her marriage to someone of a lower social order. She was totally committed to the suffrage movement.

Princess Sophia Duleep Singh stated that her life was devoted to *"the advancement of women"*. She became a nurse in the First World War and nursed many Indian soldiers who could hardly believe that they were being nursed by the granddaughter of the great Maharajah Ranjit Singh. Her activities were often an embarrassment to the King and the government and she died in 1948.

Maud Arncliffe Sennett resigned from the WFL in 1910 but continued to donate to the WSPU until commencement of its arson campaign. She disagreed with the WSPU's policy in support of the war effort and lent her support to Sylvia Pankhurst's 'East London Federation of Suffragettes'. She died from tuberculosis in September 1936 at her home in Midhurst.

Florence de Fonblanque did not feature much in the annals of the suffragettes after the Edinburgh March to London in 1912 which she organised and led and in which Sarah played a central part.

Mary Leigh, the Drum-Major of the WSPU Fife & Drum Band, who had visited Christabel Pankhurst in Paris and Emily Davison's deathbed in Epsom Hospital, died in 1978 having taken part in the first Aldermaston CND march.

Edith Garrud, the Jiu-Jitsu instructor with whom Sarah maintained contact during her final years and who witnessed the codicil in her Will, retired, together with her husband William, from their physical training establishment in 1925. Edith died in 1971 aged 91.

Mary Blathwayt, who never supported militancy and exposed the lesbian relationships within the WSPU, resigned from the Union in 1913 in protest against its move towards militancy. She died in 1962 and Eagle House, the suffragettes' sanctuary, was sold.

Dame Ethel Smyth was created Dame Commander of the Order of the British Empire in 1922 in recognition of her work as a musical composer and author. A self-confessed lesbian, the culmination of her musical career was on her 75th birthday in 1934 when her work was performed at the Royal Albert Hall in the presence of the Queen although, as the eminent conductor Leon Botstein pointed out:

> *"Heartbreakingly, at this moment of long-overdue recognition, the composer was already completely deaf and could hear neither her own music nor the adulation of the crowds."*

She died in 1944 aged 86 having acquired considerable distinction.

Dame Ethel Smyth in 1930.

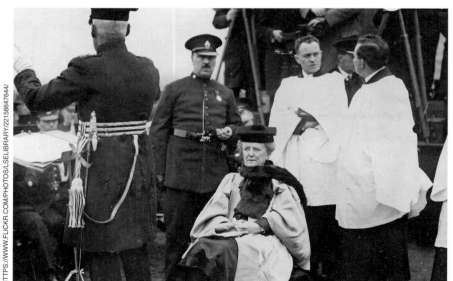

Edith Craig, daughter of actress Ellen Terry and early member of the WSPU who had sold copies of '*Votes for Women*' outside Eustace Miles's vegetarian restaurant in Chandos Place, became a prominent theatre director and producer. She lived from 1916 until her death in 1947 in a lesbian *ménage à trois* with noted painter Clare 'Tony' Atwood and the playwright, suffragette and one-time secretary to Ellen Terry, **Christabel Marshall.**

Clara Mordan became extremely rich in 1901 on the death of her father, who manufactured propelling pencils. She was one of the WSPU's most generous benefactors. Suffering from tuberculosis, she died in 1915 leaving the bulk of her fortune to Mary Allen, the woman with whom she lived.

Mabel Capper, whose mother and aunt were also WSPU members, was imprisoned six times, went on hunger strike and was forcibly fed. During the First World War she served as a nurse in the Voluntary Aid Detachment (VAD) and after the war became involved in the socialist and pacifist movements. She worked as a journalist on the '*Daily Herald*' for three years, married Cecil Chisholm in 1921 and died in 1966.

Margaret "Gretta" Cousins, who had urged women to become vegetarians and refuse to submit to cooking and household chores, moved with her husband to India in 1915 where she was involved in many aspects of women's affairs. She became the first female magistrate in India in 1922. She died in India in 1954.

Elizabeth Wolstenholme Elmy, who in 1907 inspired Sarah to renew her passion for the fight, was an honoured member of the WSPU but resigned in 1913 when she considered that its militant agenda had become a threat to human life. She was then involved in the tax resistance movement and died in 1918.

Edith How-Martyn who, in the early days of the suffrage campaign, had been arrested for attempting to make a speech in the House of Commons, resigned from the WSPU in protest against its policy of violence and later from the WFL. During the 1930s she travelled through India promoting birth control. She emigrated with her husband to Australia at the start of World War 2 and died there in 1954.

Emma Sproson (Red Emma) had joined the suffrage campaign after Lord Curzon, at a political meeting, had refused to answer her question because she was a woman. She joined and left both the WSPU and the WFL in protest of what she considered their autocratic management style. She became Wolverhampton's first female councillor in 1921 and died in 1936.

Margaret Nevinson was one of the founder members of the WFL in 1907. Her marriage to the radical journalist Henry Nevinson was not a success and the couple ended up eating in separate rooms. After World War 1 she continued to campaign for women's rights and wrote a two-volume autobiography. She died, an unhappy woman, in 1932.

Anne Cobden-Sanderson, another founder of the WFL, was three years younger than Sarah and, together with her husband, founded the Doves Press which, among other works, published the Doves Bible using the Doves typeface which it had developed. When imprisoned in 1906, she was released following a protest by George Bernard Shaw. She died in 1926.

Helena Normanton, another WFL founder, was an eminent King's Counsel (KC) and campaigned throughout her life for women's rights. She was the first married woman to be granted a passport in her maiden name; the first woman to practise as a barrister in England; the first woman to obtain a divorce for her client and the first woman to prosecute in a murder trial. She was a lifelong pacifist and campaigned for nuclear disarmament after World War 2. She died in 1957.

Ada Wright, was the woman whose photograph, collapsed on the ground, appeared on the front page of the *'Daily Mirror'* after 'Black Friday'. It became an iconic image of the brutal treatment the suffragettes received from police and public alike. During World War 1 she drove an ambulance, groomed horses and worked in canteens. A wealthy woman, she died in 1939 leaving several generous bequests to other suffragettes including £1,600 to Christabel Pankhurst and £200 to Flora Drummond.

Isabel Cowe, the gallant lady from St. Abbs Head who had taken such an active part in the march from Edinburgh, waged an ongoing war with her parish council over rates, rubbish collection and the condition of the roads. She died in 1931 and a sun dial was erected at her house in her memory by the many people who had come to know and respect her.

Margaret Byham, one of the six Edinburgh marchers who, like Sarah, completed the full course, accompanied Florence de Fonblanque to the door of Number 10, Downing Street, to hand in their petition. She died in Chichester in 1960 aged 94.

Ruth Cavendish Bentinck, WFL and former WSPU member, undertook part of the Edinburgh March in 1912. Afterwards, with Florence de Fonblanque, she founded 'The Qui Vive Corps' intended as an early response flying squad of suffrage protestors which never really came to much. She died in 1953.

Mary Richardson, the suffragette who slashed 'The Rokeby Venus' in the National Gallery, helped Sylvia Pankhurst in the East End during World War 1 after which she stood three times, unsuccessfully, as a Labour parliamentary candidate. She then joined the 'British Union of Fascists' in which she became a leading member. She died in1961.

Gertrude Mary Ansell crowned her record of imprisonments, hunger strikes and forced feedings for WSPU activities with a 6-month prison sentence in May 1914. This was for vandalising Herkomer's painting of the Duke of Wellington in the Royal Academy but she was released on the amnesty. She was also heavily involved with animal rights and the anti-vivisection movement. She was force fed 236 times and died in 1932 following an operation for gallstones.

Daisy Parsons left the WSPU for Sylvia Pankhurst's ELFS and worked during World War 1 setting up a Mother and Child Welfare Centre in West Ham to help women whose husbands were at the front. She then moved into local politics and became Mayor of West Ham in 1931 and a Justice of the Peace in 1933. In World War 2 she organised the evacuation of children and the organisation of the Women's Voluntary Service (WVS) in the East End. She died in 1957.

Rosa May Billinghurst 'The Cripple Suffragette' took part in the full range of WSPU militancy, despite her disability, and was imprisoned several times and suffered force feeding. She transferred to the WFL and gave up campaigning after the war but attended Emmeline Pankhurst's funeral and the unveiling of her memorial in 1930. She died in 1953.

Jessie Chrystal Macmillan, the first female science graduate from the University of Edinburgh, was a delegate at the 'Women's International Peace Congress' at The Hague in 1915. After the war she served as a delegate at the 'Paris Peace Conference 1919', and encouraged the founding of the 'League of Nations'. She was called to the Bar in 1924 and as a barrister fought relentlessly for women's equality. She died in 1937.

Emily Hobhouse, who had gained fame for her work in exposing the South African concentration camps, opposed the war and in 1915 wrote the 'Open Christmas Letter' addressed *"To the Women of Germany and Austria"*. After the war she raised large sums to fight starvation among women and children in Central Europe. She was regarded as a heroine in South Africa and when she died in 1926 her ashes were placed in a niche in the National Women's Monument at Bloemfontein. A town was named 'Hobhouse' after her and in 1971 a submarine of the South African Navy was named *SAS Emily Hobhouse*, in her honour. In 1994 it was renamed *SAS Umkhonto*.

Rosa Meyreder the Austrian author, and feminist who responded favourably to Hobhouse's 'Open Christmas Letter' was actively engaged

HTTP://WWW.SAVINGSUTHERLAND.ORG.UK/HOSPITAL.HTM

King George V and Queen Mary inspecting the Duchess of Sutherland's hospital in France during World War 1

in the peace movement throughout the war and in 1919 became chairman of the *Internationale Frauenliga für Frieden und Freiheit* (International Women's League for Peace and Liberty, IFFF). She died in Vienna in 1938.

Lida Gustava Heymann, the German pacifist and campaigner for women's rights, demanded the expulsion of Adolf Hitler from Germany in 1923 but had wisely left the country for Switzerland before he came to power ten years later. She died in Zürich in 1943 aged 75.

Aletta Henriëtte Jacobs, was the first woman to qualify as a doctor in the Netherlands but in 1899 she stopped practising to concentrate on women's rights and suffrage. In 1915 she was the prime mover in establishing the 'International Women's Congress' at The Hague and continued promoting the feminist cause until her death in 1929 aged 75.

Clemence Annie Housman, sister of A. E. Housman and Laurence Housman, all well known authors, was also an ardent suffragette and WSPU member. She was a committee member of the 'Women's Tax Resistance League' and was arrested for non-payment of taxes in 1911 and imprisoned for a short time in Holloway. She died in 1955.

Beatrice Harraden was another author whose first novel, '*Ships that Pass in the Night*', became a best seller. She was a member of the WSPU and of the 'Women's Tax Resistance League'. She received a civil list pension in 1930 in recognition of her literary work and died in 1936.

Millicent Leveson-Gower, the beautiful Duchess of Sutherland who worked with Sarah to combat deaths from lead poisoning in the Potteries, established a Field Ambulance in Belgium on the outbreak of the First World War. She was trapped for six weeks behind enemy lines but managed to escape back to England. She moved her unit to France and at the end of the war was awarded the French *Croix de Guerre*, the Belgian *Royal Red Cross*, and the British *Red Cross Medal*. After the death of the 4th Duke, she married again twice, both of which marriages were unfortunate: her second husband was an adulterer and her third a homosexual. She later wrote a semi-autobiographical novel entitled *That Fool of a Woman*. She was living in France on the outbreak of World War 2 and was captured by the Germans but escaped through Spain and Portugal to the United States. She returned to France after the war where she died in 1955. Her ashes were interred at Dunrobin Castle, Sutherland.

The house in Chester Terrace where Sarah was born and spent her early years is still a private residence. Fritham House in the New Forest is today a care home for the elderly and St. Andrews in Lyme Regis has been converted by its present owners into a six-bedroom house and seven flats. The house in Burslem where Sarah lived during her years in the Potteries escaped the enemy bombing in World War 2 and looks much the same today as it did in her time. The houses in Hampstead and Finchley where she lived in later years are both still standing and in private ownership.

Holy Trinity Church in Marylebone where Sarah was christened, and giggled through the service with her sisters when their mother was not there, fell into disuse in the 1930s and is today an event venue hosting some 100 events each year including exhibitions, marriages, press launches and corporate dinners.

The New Forest Union Workshop, where Sarah developed her early ambitions to be of service to the poor and needy, was taken over by Southampton County Council in the 1930s and used as a Public Assistance Institution. Today it is an NHS property known as the Ashurst Hospital.

Anderton's Hotel where in 1907 Sarah listened to Flora Drummond speaking and had her first thoughts about becoming a suffragette, is today lost behind the modern frontage of the Fleet Street Commercial Centre. The WSPU Headquarters in Kingsway is 'Bill's Holborn Restaurant' serving breakfast, lunch and dinner from 8 am to 10 pm daily

Holloway Prison, the largest women's prison in Western Europe, became, and remains, a linchpin in the story of the fight for women's suffrage. Sarah knew it well as did many other suffragettes and at least one period of suffering within its walls became *de rigeur* for serious suffrage campaigners. In recent years, there were several inquiries by the Prison Service following allegations of bullying, sexual harassment, theft and inadequate hygiene and safety standards and in September 2016 the prisoners were moved out to other facilities and Holloway Prison was closed. The site is to be sold but at the time of writing its future use has yet to be decided.

Sarah's other place of incarceration, Winson Green Prison in Birmingham, became in 2011 the first British prison to be transferred from the Prison Service to a private management company but in December 2016 the outbreak of serious rioting necessitated the summoning of specialist riot squads from H. M. Prison Service to restore order. Some £2 million worth of damage was done during the riots and it was claimed that drugs, overcrowding and shortage of prison staff had been at the root of the problems.

The Caxton Hall, formerly the Westminster Town Hall, on the corner of Palmer Street and Caxton Street, will be remembered by many for its

Rebel with a Cause

role in the postwar years as a registry office in which a number of important people, and theatrical celebrities, were married in civil ceremonies. In 1979 the registry office was closed and the building lay empty until its conversion into thirteen luxury flats in 2006. The back of the building which contained the two halls, the Great Hall and the York Hall, was demolished and an office block built on the site. These halls had played host to a number of important events since they were first opened in 1883: Winston Churchill held press conferences here during World War 2; and in 1940, Sir Michael O'Dwyer, former Lieutenant Governor of the Punjab, was assassinated here by an Indian nationalist for his part in the *Jallianwala Bagh* massacre at Amritsar in 1919.

But perhaps its most well-known function was as the meeting place for the suffragettes of the WSPU. It was here on 13th February 1907, to coincide with the opening of Parliament, that the WSPU held their first 'Women's Parliament' and the following month on 20th March the second, at which Sarah reported for her first operation as a suffragette. It was from here that she set out leading her three unruly followers from Preston to face the wall of policemen which confronted them.

A stone's throw from the Hall, at a point over which Sarah and her legion of impassioned women almost certainly passed as they battled their way through to Victoria Street, is a small garden, the Chichester Garden, in the

north-west corner of which stands a memorial to those women. It is a bronze scroll, symbolising the petitions which the suffragettes so frequently and so unsuccessfully attempted to present to Parliament, commissioned by the 'Suffragette Fellowship' and designed by Edwin Russel.

It was unveiled in 1970 in the presence of a few of the still remaining suffragettes and several dignitaries including Baroness Edith

Baroness Edith Clara Summerskill, Member of Parliament, physician and lifelong fighter for women's rights.

Summerskill, Labour politician, physician, feminist and lifelong fighter for women's rights. During the 1950s Dr. Summerskill entered into a correspondence with her daughter, Shirley, who also became a physician and Member of Parliament and was an ardent feminist like her mother. In these, Summerskill stated her belief that women are superior to men in almost every way – stronger physically, tougher emotionally and equal, if not superior, intellectually. In one of the letters she summarised the difficulties which women had faced in obtaining recognition in academic and public life:

> *"The insistent demand of women for recognition in spheres of work outside the home, which has quietly but unremittingly been advanced in the course of the last hundred years, has grudgingly been conceded. As a doctor and a Member of Parliament I am fully conscious of the fact that the doors both of the medical schools and of the House of Commons had to be forced by furious and frustrated women before their claims were recognized. It would be quite inaccurate to suggest that we were welcomed into the universities or into public life."* [55]

At the unveiling of the memorial in Chichester Garden, Baroness Summerskill spoke emotionally of the debt which women owed to the suffragettes and pledged that she, herself, would try to make some contribution to the women's cause.

Also at the unveiling was Labour politician Dr. Horace King, Speaker of the House of Commons, later Baron Maybray-King of the City of Southampton. He also spoke of the way that, thanks largely to the suffragettes, women had won acceptance in almost every profession. He even went as far as to make the outrageously fanciful prediction that, in his opinion, sooner or later, there would be a woman Prime Minister of the United Kingdom.

APPENDIX 'A'

Chronology of Principal Events
in the Fight for Women's Rights and Suffrage

1817 First Appeal for Equality for Women
by Jeremy Bentham
"Plan of Parliamentary Reform in the form of a Catechism."

1825 Continuation of Bentham's Appeal for Equality for Women
by William Thompson and Anna Wheeler
"An Appeal of One Half the Human Race, Women, Against the Pretensions of the Other Half, Men, to Retain Them in Political, and Thence in Civil and Domestic Slavery: In Reply to Mr. Mill's Celebrated Article on Government."
(James Mills had suggested that women's interests were always incorporated in those of their fathers or their husbands and need not therefore be addressed separately.)

1832 FIRST REFORM ACT (Representation of the People Act 1832)
Extended the franchise with property qualifications to include small landowners, tenant farmers, and shopkeepers in the boroughs and to all householders in the towns who paid a yearly rental of £10 or more. Inclusion of the word 'male' specifically excluded women.

1850 *Birth of Sarah Benett.*

1867 SECOND REFORM ACT (Representation of the People Act 1867)
Extended the franchise further by relaxing property qualifications thereby doubling the number of male adults with the vote from one million to two million in a population of about seven million.

Petition for inclusion of women presented by **John Stewart Mill**.

National Society for Women's Suffrage (NSWS) formed in Manchester by **Lydia Becker** and in London by **Millicent Garrett Fawcett**.

1869 MUNICIPAL FRANCHISE ACT
Gave the right to vote, in local elections only, to single women who were ratepayers.

1884 THIRD REFORM ACT (Representation of the People Act 1884)
Levelled the property qualifications between town and country thereby increasing male voters to around 60% of the population.
Amendment to include women was rejected.

1889 Women's Franchise League (WFL)
formed by **Richard and Emmeline Pankhurst** but disagreement between members and hostility with the NSWS result in its folding after the first year.

1894 LOCAL GOVERNMENT ACT
Extended the right to vote in local elections to certain married women who were also permitted to become poor law guardians, and to act on school boards.

Sarah Benett moves to Burslem in the Potteries.

1897 Formation of National Union of Women's Suffrage Societies (NUWSS) from twenty regional groups which agreed to speak with a single voice. **Millicent Garrett Fawcett** elected President.
The NUWSS was a democratic body dedicated to gaining the vote for women through peaceful and lawful means. For the next several years it introduced a number of petitions and Parliamentary Bills. All were rejected.

1903 Women's Social and Political Union (WSPU)
formed by **Emmeline Pankhurst** in Manchester. Its aims were to campaign aggressively for equal rights for women in unofficial partnership with the **Independent Labour Party (ILP)**.
Membership was restricted to women.

1905 WOMEN'S FRANCHISE BILL
introduced by **John Bamford Slack MP** 'talked out' and abandoned.
WSPU commence militant campaign and break ties with ILP which now supports universal suffrage. First WSPU militancy – Christabel Pankhurst and Annie Kenney arrested and imprisoned.

1906 **HQ of WSPU moves to London. Militant protests start in earnest.**
Liberal Government returned with huge majority.

1907 **First 'Women's Parliament' in Caxton Hall.**
Sarah Benett's First Arrest and Imprisonment
'The Split' – **Women's Freedom League (WFL)** formed in protest against the Pankhursts' autocratic management of WSPU.
Sarah, with others, moves from WSPU to WFL.

1908 **Herbert Asquith becomes Prime Minister.**
Sarah Benett's Second Arrest and Imprisonment.
Elizabeth Garrett Anderson becomes first female Mayor in Britain.
Sarah Benett appointed Hon. Treasurer of WFL.
Women's Tax Resistance League (WTRL) founded.

1909 **Dissolution of Parliament.**
First Hunger Strikes by Suffragettes. Forced feeding introduced.
Formation of **National League for Opposing Woman Suffrage (NLOWS)** with Lord Cromer as first president.

1910 **FIRST CONCILIATION BILL** to extend women's suffrage.
WSPU agree to truce on militancy during passage of Bill.
Election intervened and Bill dropped. Militancy restarts.
King George V succeeds King Edward VII (6 May)
'Black Friday' (18 Nov.) WSPU demonstration met by police brutality.
Liberals returned with greatly reduced majority (19 Dec.)
Sarah disillusioned with feeble tactics of WFL returns to WSPU.

1911 **SECOND CONCILIATION BILL.** Further WSPU truce during passage. Bill passes second reading with large majority but is sabotaged and dropped. Militancy resumed. Suffragettes boycott National Census.
Great Coronation Procession of 40,000 women, 5 miles long.
Sarah's Third Arrest and Imprisonment.

1912 **PARLIAMENTARY FRANCHISE (WOMEN) BILL**
(Third Conciliation Bill) defeated by 208 to 222.
Sarah's Fourth Arrest and Imprisonment for breaking windows.

Pethick-Lawrences expelled from WSPU. Christabel Pankhurst flees to Paris. Labour Party backs NUWSS in support of women's suffrage.

Sarah completes 400 mile Edinburgh to London March.

1913 **FRANCHISE AND REGISTRATION BILL** with amendment for women's suffrage dropped following Speaker's ruling. WSPU respond by stepping up bomb and arson attacks.

Sarah's Fifth Arrest and Imprisonment (breaking Selfridge's windows).

CAT AND MOUSE ACT (Prisoners (Temporary Discharge for Ill Health) Act) introduced.
Emily Wilding Davison killed under King's horse at Epsom Derby. Huge funeral procession in London. Mrs. Pankhurst arrested and goes on hunger strike
WSPU's new HQs in Kingsway raided by police. Several arrests.

Sarah's Sixth Arrest and Imprisonment in Birmingham.

1914 **Slashing of paintings by WSPU members.**
Sylvia Pankhurst splits from WSPU and forms East London Federation of Suffragettes (ELFS).
March to Buckingham Palace to present petition to King.

Sarah's Seventh and Final Arrest and Imprisonment (as 'Susan Burnton'). Released under Cat and Mouse Act and re-arrested.

WAR DECLARED (4 August)
All suffrage prisoners released. Militant action ceases.

1915 **WOMEN'S PEACE CONGRESS AT THE HAGUE**
Over 1,200 delegates from 14 countries attend.
Women's International League for Peace and Freedom founded.

1916 **SPEAKER'S CONFERENCE** agrees that a recommendation should go forward that women over the age of 30, subject to certain qualifications, should be given the vote.

Sarah Benett organises pilgrimage to the grave of Emily Davison in Morpeth, Northumberland.

From 1914-1918 women undertake many forms of war work. Suffrage campaigners split into two factions – WSPU-led group support the war, back the Government and encourage enlistment; NUWSS-led group predominantly anti-war, many encourage pacifism and peace initiatives. Millicent Fawcett pledges to back the Government.

1918 **REPRESENTATION OF THE PEOPLE ACT 1918**
Recommendations of the Speaker's Conference accepted. Franchise extended to all men over 21, or 19 if they had military service, and women over 30 with minimal status qualifications. Electorate tripled to 21.4 million 43% of whom were women.

PARLIAMENT (QUALIFICATION OF WOMEN) ACT 1918
gives women over 21 the right to stand for election as an MP (though they still could not vote until they were 30)

1919 Nancy Astor becomes first woman MP to sit at Westminster.

1924 *Death of Sarah Benett.*

1928 **REPRESENTATION OF THE PEOPLE (EQUAL FRANCHISE) ACT 1928**
Universal Suffrage at last! Women are given the vote on equal terms with men, at the age of 21.

1969 **REPRESENTATION OF THE PEOPLE ACT 1969**
lowered the voting age from 21 to 18, with effect from 1970.

APPENDIX 'B'

Footnotes

1   *"Bradshaw's Handbook to London"* 1891.

2   Sarah Benett *"My Imprisonments"* MS in private ownership.

3   Barbara Benett (*née* Waring) Annuary 1843-75 MS
      Lyme Regis Museum.

4   Sarah Barbara Benett *Diary* 1860-July 1862 MS
      Lyme Regis Museum.

5   *"The Vote"* Saturday 6th March 1910, Page 220.

6   Constance Purvis *"Memories of Lyme"* MS
      Lyme Regis Museum.

7   Last Will and Testament of William Morgan Benett.

8   W. R. Lee *"British Journal of Industrial Medicine"*
      5th November 1963.

9   John Ward *"The Borough of Stoke-upon-Trent at the Commencement of the Reign of Queen Victoria"* 1843.

10   *"The Staffordshire Advertiser"* 4th September 1842.

11   Samuel Scriven *"Report to H M Commissioners on the employment of Children and Young Persons in the District of the Staffordshire Potteries"* 1841.

12   Arnold Benett *"Clayhanger"* 1910.

13   Harold Owen *"The Staffordshire Potter"* 1901.

14   Sarah Benett *"The Co-operative News"* September 1900.

15   *"London Daily News"* 21st March 1907.

16   Letter from Lloyd George to C P Scott, 29 November 1909.
      Quoted by John D Clare johndclare.net

17   Quoted by Sarah Gristwood, *"Winston versus the Women"* Huffpost.

18   Sarah Benett *"The Vote"* 25th November 1909.

19   *"Hansard"* 13th March 1912, vol 35 cc1097-8.

20   *"Pall Mall Gazette"* 29th March 1912.

21   Emmeline Pethick-Lawrence *"My Part in a Changing World"* 1938.

22   *"The Globe"* 27th July 1912.

23   *"Pall Mall Gazette"* 15th June 1912.

24   *"Berwick Journal"* October 1912.

25   *"Hendon and Finchley Times"* 22nd November 1912.

26   *'The Scotsman'* 18th November 1912.

27   Emmeline Pankhurst in a speech at a WSPU Meeting in Cardiff February 1913.

28   *"Nottingham Journal"* 22nd July 1913.

29   *"The Times"* 11th March 1914.

30   Statement by Mary Wood read at WSPU Meeting in Knightbridge Hall, May 1914.

31   *"The Woman's Dreadnought"* Journal of the ELFS, May 1914.

32   Quoted at the East London Suffragette Festival. August 2004, commemorating the centenary of the foundation of the ELFS.

33   *"Daily Telegraph"* 22nd May 1914.

34   *"Hull Daily Mail"* 25th May 1914.

35   Emmeline Pankhurst *"My Own Story"* 1914.

36   *"Jus Suffragii"* Journal of the International Woman Suffrage Alliance 1st March 1918.

37   *"The Suffragette"* 16th April 1915.

38   *"Women at the Hague, the International Congress of Women and its Results"* 1915 Page 10.

39   Beatrice Harraden quoted in *"We Won't Pay!"* 2008 Page 325.

40   Quoted in poster advertising a Mass Meeting in Edinburgh of The Northern Men's Federation for Women's Suffrage 14th November 1914, National Library of Scotland.

41   Women Suffrage Campaigners: Millicent Fawcett, www.parliament.uk

42   *"Hansard"* House of Commons Debates, 22nd May 1917.

43   Letter from Edward de Mussenden Leathes 1994, Purvis Family Papers.

44   Letter from Ivy Morgan (*née* de Mussenden Leathes) 1994, Purvis Family Papers.

45   *"The Vote"* 29th February 1924.

46   George Bernard Shaw at a Meeting ofthe NTRL October 1913 Quoted in *"The Green Bag: an Entertaining Magazine for Lawyers"*, March 1913.

47   Article in *"The Times"* Quoted in *"The Green Bag: an Entertaining Magazine for Lawyers"*, March 1913.

48   Entry in the diary of Millicent Garrett Fawcett 2nd July 1928 Quoted in www.spartacus-educational.com

49   Millicent Garrett Fawcett in an article in *"The Times"* 1906 Quoted in *"Queen Christabel"* by David Mitchell 1977.

50   Millicent Garrett Fawcett in an article in *"The Manchester Guardian"* 22nd August 1912.

51   David Lloyd George speaking in 1913 quoted in *"Did the Suffragettes Help"* johndclare.net

52   *"Hansard"* 28th March 1912, debate on Parliamentary Franchise (Women) Bill.

53   *"Morning Post"* 2nd March 1912.

54   Annie Kenney *"Memories of a Militant"* 1924.

55   Shirley Summerskill *"Letters to my Daughter"* 1957.

APPENDIX 'C'

Acknowledgements and Principal Sources Consulted

I am grateful to a number of people who have helped me in the reconstruction of Sarah Benett's life. Firstly, and most importantly, to John Purvis, Sarah's great-grand nephew, for asking me to undertake the book and entrusting me with Sarah's manuscript and other papers. I had previously written biographies of two of John's illustrious Purvis forebears but both were on naval and military subjects, which are my specialities. However, to entrust me with the biography of a suffragette, a subject of which I knew nothing, was a vote of faith for which I am truly grateful.

In researching and writing this book I have become properly aware of the enormous debt which the world owes to the suffragists for their part in releasing half the population of the western world from the monstrous subjugation it had suffered for so long from the other half. I hope that in offering a reasonably one-dimensional look at the subject, which does not plunge into the depths of scholarly enquiry and analysis, I may make others, like myself, aware of the nobility of the Cause and the sacrifice and commitment of the women who fought for it.

John's father, William Hugh Allen Purvis, deposited a substantial tranche of his family papers, relating to the Benett and Waring families, to the Museum in Lyme Regis where both families had their roots. I am grateful to the Museum for giving me access to these papers, and to Richard Bull in particular for his enthusiasm and help in digging out documents and photographs some of which are reproduced in this book.

For their help in my research I must thank Anne Cotterson-Smith, Parish Administrator and Jenny Hall, Local Historian of Warborough, Oxfordshire;

Sophie Stewart, National Cooperative Archivist; Dr. Wayne Phillips; Sarah Soames of Savills; Andrew Thomas of the Crown Estates; Natalya Thomas of Getty Images; Ian Porter of 'London Town Walks' and Eric Duke Scott for the material on his parents.

As usual, I am indebted to my publisher, Brigadier Henry Wilson, my wife, Anthea, for her copy-editing and my dear friends Natalie Gilbert and Squadron Leader Adrian Richardson for their encouragement and help. I also gratefully but sadly record the assistance of Dr. Adrian Pilling, who died tragically early at the age of 68 in September 2017. Adrian travelled all over Europe with me researching battlefields and military sites and, together with his colleague Dr. Keith Daniels, gave me valuable medical insight in certain matters relating to my subjects. He was a stalwart friend and is sorely missed.

Internet Sources

For any writer today, the wonderful **Wikipedia** has become the inestimable source of information offering authoritative commentary and guidance for further research on an unbelievably wide range of subjects. I have used it extensively and also its sister organisation **Wikimedia Commons** where one may obtain images which are in the public domain and free of copyright restrictions. I have included several of these in this book and sincerely hope I have attributed them correctly; I think I have but if I have inadvertently breached any existing copyright, I apologise to the holder and would ask them to contact me through my publishers.

Other than Wikipedia, there are several internet sites with access to information on women's rights. Among those I have consulted are:

www.spartacus-educational.com free online access to a very wide range of well-informed articles on British, European and American history.

www.parliament.uk all aspects of the UK parliamentary system and access to the parliamentary archives.

www.hansard.millbanksystems.com transcriptions of historic debates in both Houses of Parliament.

www.britishnewspaperarchive.co.uk the largest online collection of British and Irish historical newspapers (fees apply).

www.bl.uk/sisterhood/timeline the British Library. Excellent timeline of progress of women's rights since 1960.

www.nationalarchives.gov.uk information on the source of many original documents concerned with women's suffrage.

Unpublished Sources

The Purvis Papers, Sarah Benett's manuscript *"My Imprisonments"*, her arrest and prison release documents and various other papers. In the possession of the family.

Lyme Regis Museum, Diaries, Annuaries, Photographs and other papers relating to the Benett and Waring families.

Published Sources and Selected Bibliography

Anderson, Louisa Garrett, *Elizabeth Garrett Anderson* (Faber 1939)

Balfour, Betty, (Editor) *Letters of Constance Lytton* (Heinemann 1925)

Bartley, Paula, *Votes for Women 1860-1928* (Hodder & Stoughton 1998)

Collis, Louise, *Impetuous Heart: the story of Ethel Smyth* (William Kimber 1984)

Crawford, Elizabeth, *The Women's Suffrage Movement: a Reference Guide 1866-1928* (UCL Press 1999).

Fulford, Roger, *Votes for Women: the story of a struggle* (Faber & Faber 1957)

Housman, Laurence, *The Unexpected Years* (Jonathan Cape 1937)

John, Angela, & Eustance, Claire, (Editors) *The Men's Share? Masculinities, Male Support and Women's Suffrage in Britain, 1890-1920* (Routledge 1997)

Kenney, Annie, *Memories of a Militant* (Edward Arnold 1924)

Lansbury, George, *My Life* (Constable 1928)

Lytton, Constance Bulwer, (*aka* Jane Warton) *Prisons and Prisoners,* George H. Doran, New York, 1914

McPhee, Carol & Fitzgerald, Ann, (Editors) *The Non-Violent Militant: Selected Writings of Teresa Billington-Greig* (Routledge 1987)

Nevinson, Henry, *The Fire of Life* (James Nisbet 1935)

Pankhurst, Christabel, *Unshackled: the story of how we won the Vote* (Hutchinson 1959)

Pankhurst, Emmeline, *My Own Story* (Eveleigh Nash 1914)

Pankhurst, Sylvia, *The Suffragette Movement: an intimate account of persons and ideals* (Longmans 1931)

— *The Life of Emmeline Pankhurst* (Houghton Miflin, Boston & New York 1936).

Pethick-Lawrence, Emmeline, *My Part in a Changing World* (Victor Gollancz 1938)

Pugh, Martin, *The March of the Women: a Revisionist Analysis of the Campaign for Women's Suffrage, 1866-1914* (Oxford University Press 2000)

Purvis, June, *Emmeline Pankhurst: a Biography* (Routledge 2002).

Rosen, Andrew, *Rise Up Women! The Militant Campaign of the Women's Social and Political Union 1903-1914* (Routledge & Kegan Paul 1974)

Smyth, Ethel, *Female Pipings in Eden* (Peter Davies 1933)

Stanley Liz & Morley, Ann, *The Life and Death of Emily Wilding Davison* (Women's Press 1988)

Thompson, Margaret & Mary, *They Couldn't Stop Us! The Experiences of Two (usually law-abiding) Women* (Ancient House Press 1957)

Descendants of Captain Charles Cowper Benett, Royal Navy, c.1788-1877 and his wife Sarah Burlton 1792-1853

William Charles
BENETT
Bengal Civil Service
1844-1922

Margaret Waring
BENETT
1845-1925
m.1881 Arthur
Knatchbull
CONNELL

Sarah Barbara
BENETT
1846-1905
m.1868 James
Henry
ALLEN

Mary Jane
BENETT
1847-1907
m.1874 Albert
Reginald
GRAVES

Etheldred
Margaret
ALLEN
1869-1913

William
Jeffreys Benett
ALLEN
Major RFA
1870-1921
died in India

Constance Augusta
Burlton **ALLEN**
1872-1955
m.1904 Charles
Hugh **PURVIS**
1867-1917

Arthur Henry
Burlton
ALLEN
1872-1963
m.1910 Mary
ONSLOW

Katherine Ba
ALLEN
b.1875

Katherine Barbara
"Kitty"
PURVIS
1905-1981

Margaret Constance
PURVIS
1908-1976

William Hugh Allen
PURVIS
1915-1997
m.1958 Rosalyn P
MASTERS

Gwendolene Lou
PURVIS
1917-1995

William John
PURVIS
b.1962
m.1988 Janet
WHITE
1 daughter, 1 son

Ann
PURVIS
b.1965
m.1990 Ian
HATTON
1 son, 1 daughter

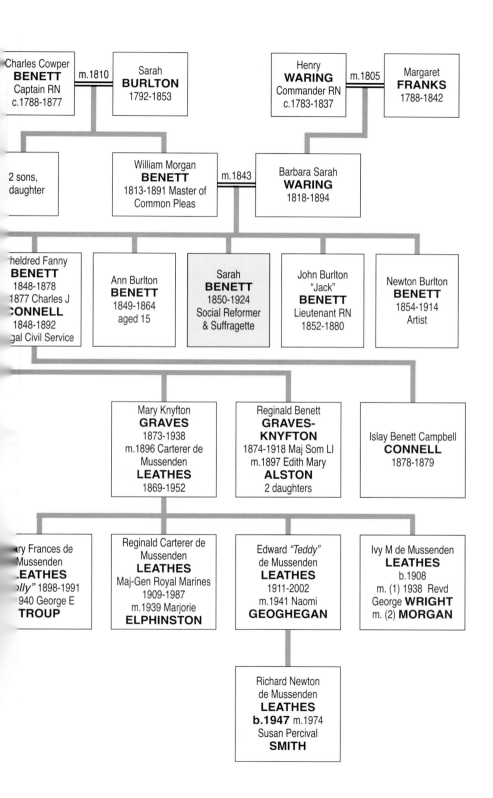

Charles Cowper
BENETT
Captain RN
c.1788-1877

m.1810

Sarah
BURLTON
1792-1853

Henry
WARING
Commander RN
c.1783-1837

m.1805

Margaret
FRANKS
1788-1842

2 sons,
daughter

William Morgan
BENETT
1813-1891 Master of
Common Pleas

m.1843

Barbara Sarah
WARING
1818-1894

heldred Fanny
BENETT
1848-1878
1877 Charles J
CONNELL
1848-1892
gal Civil Service

Ann Burlton
BENETT
1849-1864
aged 15

Sarah
BENETT
1850-1924
Social Reformer
& Suffragette

John Burlton
"Jack"
BENETT
Lieutenant RN
1852-1880

Newton Burlton
BENETT
1854-1914
Artist

Mary Knyfton
GRAVES
1873-1938
m.1896 Carterer de
Mussenden
LEATHES
1869-1952

Reginald Benett
**GRAVES-
KNYFTON**
1874-1918 Maj Som LI
m.1897 Edith Mary
ALSTON
2 daughters

Islay Benett Campbell
CONNELL
1878-1879

ary Frances de
Mussenden
LEATHES
olly" 1898-1991
940 George E
TROUP

Reginald Carterer de
Mussenden
LEATHES
Maj-Gen Royal Marines
1909-1987
m.1939 Marjorie
ELPHINSTON

Edward *"Teddy"*
de Mussenden
LEATHES
1911-2002
m.1941 Naomi
GEOGHEGAN

Ivy M de Mussenden
LEATHES
b.1908
m. (1) 1938 Revd
George **WRIGHT**
m. (2) **MORGAN**

Richard Newton
de Mussenden
LEATHES
b.1947 m.1974
Susan Percival
SMITH

Index

Index